Introduction to Medical English

医療英語入門──医療の現場から日常のシーンまで

SHOHAKUSHA

はしがき

　本テキスト『医療英語入門―医療の現場から日常のシーンまで』は、医療系の学生の皆さん、そして英語を基礎から復習する機会を必要としている学生の皆さんに活用していただけることをねらいとしたものです。

　テキストは医療従事者が必要とする場面を14のユニットで構成したものであり、その内容は、医療の現場で使われる重要な英語表現に重点を置きつつ、患者さんにただ指示を与えるだけでなく、患者さんが前向きに治療に専念できるように励ましの言葉を与えるなど、心の交流を大切にしたダイアログになるよう心がけました。病気や怪我で通院や入院をした経験のある人なら誰でも、医療に携わる方々の寄り添う姿勢に救われたことがあるのではないでしょうか。筆者自身の経験からも、それを強く感じてまいりましたし、ダイアログを作成するにあたり、お世話になった方々の言葉や表情が心に浮かんできました。また、副題が示していますように、海外旅行でも実際に必要となる英会話を含め、私たちが日常経験する様々なシーンで役立つ表現を取り入れたことも、本テキストの特徴の一つであります。

　そして、実際に海外の医療の現場でも活躍されている徳永瑞子氏によるコラムは、特に医療の現場で働くことを目指そうとする学生の皆さんにとって、何よりも大きなメッセージとなることでしょう。徳永氏は、筆者の母の友人でもあり、そのようなご縁から、幸いにも筆者はアフリカでの医療活動に関する様々なエピソードを拝聴する機会に恵まれ、氏の看護への情熱と温かさに心を動かされました。徳永氏には、ご多忙の中、本テキストの意図を汲んでいただき、貴重なコラムを寄せていただきましたことを、この場をお借りしまして、心より感謝申し上げます。最後になりましたが、本テキストの刊行にあたり、松柏社の森有紀子氏には、いつも励まし続けていただき、また、筆者の考えに十分な理解を示してくださり、的確な御助言を賜りましたことを深謝いたします。

　本テキストが、学生の皆さんの英語力の向上の一助となることを願ってやみません。

本書の使い方

　まずはじめに、**Dialogue** を聴いて、大意を掴むよう試みてください。そして、**Vocabulary Check** のコーナーで、重要語句の意味を確認しましたら、もう一度 **Dialogue** に戻り、音声を聴きながら内容の確認を進めましょう。次に、**Dialogue** の中の重要表現や文法項目を重点的に学んでいきます。その方法は、ディクテーション、英作文、リピートの練習など、内容の理解を深められるように様々なエクササイズを用意しています。また、**Useful Expressions** のコーナーでは、各 Unit のテーマに関連する表現を練習できるように工夫いたしました。そして、ペアになってロールプレイの練習を通して、自然と口をついて出てくるまで何度も声に出して練習してください。全ての Unit ではありませんが、日常会話編、**Everyday Conversation** を設けています。ここでも、同様に **Dialogue** とエクササイズを通して、皆さんに楽しく学習を進めていただきたいと思います。巻末も充実させた内容となっていますので、**Glossary** を活用して語彙力を定着させたり、他にも医療英語の表現集を参考にして、難しい用語も何度も確認するようにしてください。さあ、それでは『医療英語入門』の扉を開きましょう！

Contents

	医療の現場
Unit 1	受診の予約
Unit 2	受診
Unit 3	問診・医師による診察
Unit 4	薬の服用
Unit 5	再受診・検査
Unit 6	胃の検査
Unit 7	検査結果・入院
Unit 8	術前・術後
Unit 9	待合室での会話
Unit 10	清拭
Unit 11	リハビリ
Unit 12	歯科治療
Unit 13	回復・退院許可・退院後の生活指導
Unit 14	退院

Glossary　80　　医療用語日英対照表　90　　不規則動詞の活用表　99

日常のシーン	
バーベキューパーティーに誘う／レストランにディナーの予約をする	07
予約したレストランでの食事	13
	22
	28
空港で目的地までの行き方を訊ねる／道案内をする	33
空港で搭乗手続きをする	39
ファーストフード店で注文する	46
	50
映画のチケットを買う／駅で切符を買う	54
ホテルでチェックインをする	58
円をドルに両替する	62
バスやタクシーに乗る	66
	70
	75

代名詞早見表　102

▼コラム執筆者紹介

徳永瑞子（とくなが・みずこ）

福岡県生まれ。助産師、看護師、上智大学教授（2011年〜）、NGO「アフリカ友の会」代表。現在も日本とアフリカを行き来しながら、積極的にアフリカでのエイズ医療活動を続けている。国立嬉野病院付属看護学院、九州大学医学部付属助産婦学校、ベルギーレオポルド王記念熱帯医学校、国立公衆衛生院、放送大学を卒業。国立東京第二病院（1970年）をはじめとした病院や海外の民間団体での勤務を経て、1993年から中央アフリカ共和国にて医療活動に従事、現在に至る。また、長崎大学教授（2003年〜2007年）、聖母大学教授（2007年）として教鞭を執る。『エチオピア日記』（1987年）、『プサマカシー』（1990年）、『ザンベ』（1993年）、『アフリカの詩』（2012年）など多数の著書があるが、なかでも『プサマカシー』は第11回読売女性ヒューマン・ドキュメンタリー大賞を受賞し（1990年）、翌年には日本テレビにて山口智子主演でテレビドラマ化される。国内外での医療活動を評価され数多くの賞を受賞、2005年にはフローレンス・ナイチンゲール記章を受章。2004年には『情熱大陸』（毎日放送）で取り上げられ、中央アフリカ共和国でのエイズ医療活動家として様々な苦難に遭遇しながらも、アフリカの窮状を訴え、現地の人々に寄り添い看護する姿勢が紹介された。

Unit 1 受診の予約

Dialogue

A = Receptionist   B = Patient

Audio 1-02

On the phone

A: Good afternoon. This is Dr. Clifford's Clinic. How may I help you?
B: Hello, my name is Richard Cook. ① <u>Is it possible to make an appointment with Dr. Clifford?</u>
A: Sure, ② <u>let me check her schedule</u>... Okay, it looks like the earliest opening is Thursday at 11:30 in the morning. Is that okay with you?
B: Yes, that's fine. I can come to the clinic Thursday morning, no problem.
A: OK, great! I just need a little more information from you. Could you tell me what you would like to see the doctor about?
B: Well, I have had a pain in my stomach for the past week.
A: I see. Any other problems?
B: No, nothing at the moment. Just my stomach.
A: All right. Then I'll make your appointment at 11:30 am on Thursday, April 22nd.
B: Okay, that's great. I'll see you on Thursday. Thank you.
A: Oh, by the way, please remember to bring your health insurance card with you.
B: Yes, of course. I'll bring it with me.

※ see the doctor 「医者の診察を受ける、病院に行く」 at the moment 「今のところ」 pretty 「大変、非常に」

Vocabulary Check 🔊 Audio 1-03

(1) ～ (11) に合う語義をそれぞれ (a) ～ (k) から選びなさい。

(1) actually　　（　）　　(2) appointment　（　）
(3) bring　　　（　）　　(4) by the way　　（　）
(5) clinic　　　（　）　　(6) insurance　　　（　）
(7) opening　　（　）　　(8) pain　　　　　（　）
(9) past　　　（　）　　(10) remember to do　（　）
(11) stomach　（　）

(a)（過ぎたばかりの）過去の	(b) ところで	(c) 保険	(d) 空き
(e) 予約	(f) 痛み	(g) 実は	(h) 診療所
(i) 忘れずに〜する	(j) 持ってくる	(k) 胃（腹部）	

 Useful Expressions

Dialogue 中の下線部①②の表現を使い、＜　＞内の語を並べ替えて、英文を完成させましょう。ただし、文頭に来る語も小文字で示しています。

(1) まだ明日のシングル一部屋を予約できるでしょうか？
　　＜it / single / tomorrow / to / room / possible / for / is / reserve / a / still＞?

(2) 私の飛行機の便を変更することは可能でしょうか。
　　＜flight / would / to / possible / reschedule / be / it / my＞?

(3) よろしければあなたの出発日をお知らせください。
　　＜departure / your / me / let / know / date＞, if possible.

(4) あなたのお手伝いをさせてください。
　　＜you / me / help / let＞.

 重要表現

Dialogue 中の下線部 (2) の let は使役動詞と言い、他にも様々な例があります。
【使役動詞】 make / let / have / get
- I **made** my son **see** a dentist.（わたしは息子を歯医者に行かせました。）
- Dr. Clifford **let** me **go** home.（クリフォード先生は私を家に帰らせてくれました。）
- I'll **have** him **call** you back.（後ほど彼に電話をかけ直させます。）
- I **had** my hair **cut** yesterday.（昨日私は髪を切りました。）＊この場合、cut は過去分詞形です。
- I finally could **get** my husband **to stop** smoking.（私はようやく夫に禁煙させることができました。）

症状を表す基本表現　　　　Audio 1-04

音声を聴いて、（　　　）に入る語を書きましょう。

(1) I (　　　) a stomachache.（胃が痛いです。）

(2) I have a (　　　) headache.（軽い頭痛がします。）

(3) I have a (　　　) throat.（のどが痛いです。）

(4) I have a bad (　　　).（せきがひどいです。）

(5) I have hay fever, so my eyes are (　　　).（花粉症なので、目がかゆいです。）

(6) I have a (　　　) of 37.5℃.（37度5分の熱があります。）

(7) I feel so (　　　) that I can hardly stand.
（ふらふらしてほとんど立っていられません。）

(8) I feel a (　　　) pain here.（ここに鈍い痛みを感じます。）

(9) I'm (　　　) from pneumonia.（肺炎にかかっています。）

(10) I (　　　) last night and still feel nauseous.（昨晩嘔吐し、まだ吐き気がします。）

(11) My ears are (　　　).（耳鳴りがします。）

(12) I'm (　　　) to this medication.（この薬にアレルギーがあります。）

 ## 電話での表現　　　　Audio 1-05

電話での会話について様々な表現を確認しましょう。

(1) Hello, this is Richard Cook of ABC Corporation. May I speak to Dr. Smith?
（もしもし、ABCコーポレーションのリチャード・クックと申します。スミス先生はいらっしゃいますか。）

(2) I'm sorry, he is on another line. Would you like to leave a message?
（申し訳ありません、別の電話に出ております。伝言はございますか？）

(3) Hold on, please. I'll put you through.
（お待ちください。おつなぎします。）

(4) I'm afraid you have the wrong number.
（番号をお間違いかと思いますが。）

(5) I'll call back later. Thank you.
（すみませんが、後ほどかけ直します。）

(6) Could you tell him to call me back at 123-4560?
（後で123-4560にかけ直すよう彼に伝えていただけますか？）

予約に関する表現　　　　　　　　　　　　　　　　　　🔊 Audio 1-06

（　　　　）に appointment または reservation のどちらかを入れ、音声を聴いて発音の練習をしましょう。

★ appointment　（日時や場所を決めて）面会の約束や病院の受診の予約
　 reservation　　（飛行機・列車・劇場などの）座席の予約、ホテルの部屋やレストランの予約

(1) I have a (　　　　　　　) for 7:00 tonight.
　（今夜7時に予約を入れています。）

(2) I need to change my (　　　　　　　) to June 20th.
　（6月20日に予約を変更する必要があります。）

(3) I have to reschedule my (　　　　　　　).
　（予約を入れ直す必要があります。）

(4) I have an (　　　　　　　) with my boss at 3:00 tomorrow.
　（上司と明日3時に会う約束をしています。）

(5) I have a (　　　　　　　) on the 9:00 flight from Narita to Rome.
　（成田発ローマ行きの9時の便を予約しています。）

 **Column**

看護師を目指すきっかけとなったエピソードなど

　私は幼少の頃、喘息で自宅療養をしていました。喘息発作を起こすたびにかかりつけの開業医に運ばれました。馴染みの看護師さんがいつも「大丈夫、大丈夫」と優しく私の背中を撫でてくれました。私はその若い看護師さんを見るととても安心しました。看護師さんは、白衣の上に真白い予防衣を着て白い靴下に白い靴をはいていました。その純白の白衣姿にも憧れました。看護師さんから、空になった医薬品の箱をもらうのが嬉しくて、その箱に私の宝物を入れて大切にしました。子どもの頃から私は看護師以外の職業は考えられませんでした。病弱な私に優しく手を差し伸べ安心感を与えてくれた看護師さんのことが今でも思い出されます。

Everyday Conversation

Inviting Friends to a Barbecue Party

Audio 1-07

A = Ms. Clifford   B = Steve   C = Lisa

On the phone

A: Hello.
B: Hello, Ms. Clifford, this is Steve. Can I speak to Lisa?
A: Sorry, she is out right now. I think she'll be back in about half an hour. Can I take a message?
B: Actually, I'm just about to go out and I think I'll be back this evening. Could you tell her that I'll call her again this evening? Maybe around 6:00.
A: Sure.
B: Thank you, Ms. Clifford. Bye.

That evening

C: Hello.
B: Hi, this is Steve.
C: Hi, Steve. It's me, Lisa. How are you?
B: I'm good, thanks. By the way, are you busy tomorrow?
C: No plans actually. I'm free.
B: Great, we're going to have a barbecue party and would like you to come. Jane and Ken also will be there.
C: Sounds nice! I'll bring an apple pie for dessert.
B: Good! Can you come to my house around noon?
C: Sure. Thank you for the invite. I'm looking forward to seeing everyone tomorrow.
B: Me, too. See you then.

※ be out「出かけている」be just about to do「今まさに〜しようとしている」have a party「パーティを開く」

True or False

(1)〜(5) の文を読み、本文の内容に合うものにはT（True）、当てはまらない場合はF（False）を[　] に書きなさい。

(1) [　] Ms. Clifford says that Lisa will be back in thirty minutes.
(2) [　] Steve wants Lisa to call him back later.
(3) [　] Lisa will be very busy tomorrow.
(4) [　] Jane will bring a pie to Steve's house.
(5) [　] Steve will pick up Lisa at her house about 12:00.

Unit 1
受診の予約

Making a Reservation

Audio 1-08

A = Receptionist B = Customer

On the phone

A: Hello, this is Bluebird Restaurant. May I help you?

B: Yes, I'd like to (①   ) a reservation for 7:00 p.m. next Friday.

A: Thank you, sir. Just a moment, please. Well, next Friday is July 4th. I'm very sorry, but unfortunately there are no tables available at 7:00 p.m. Friday is usually our (②   ) night.

B: Oh, I see. Do you have any other available tables at a later time?

A: Actually, yes, we do. How about 8:00 p.m.? There is a table (③   ) at that time.

B: That's great. I'll make the reservation for 8:00 p.m. then.

A: Certainly. For how many, sir?

B: There will be two of us.

A: Okay, a table for two on July 4th at 8:00 p.m. May I (④   ) your name, please?

B: Yes, of course. My name is Ken Nakamura.

A: Could you (⑤   ) your last name?

B: N-A-K-A-M-U-R-A. Nakamura.

A: Okay, Mr. Nakamura. And your phone number, please?

B: My number is 012-3456-7890.

※ unfortunately「あいにく」

Listening Exercise

❶ダイアログの音声を聴いて、(①   ) 〜 (⑤   ) に入る語を書きましょう。

❷音声を聴いて、(   ) に入る語を書きましょう。

Audio 1-09

(1) (   ) do you spell your name, please?（お名前の綴りを教えてください。）

(2) (   ) is your cell phone number, please?（携帯電話の番号は何番ですか。）

(3) Could I (   ) your name, please?（お名前を伺ってもよろしいですか。）

(4) Could I reserve a table (   ) (   ) tonight?
（今夜テーブル席を7名で予約したいのですが。）

(5) How many people in your (   ), sir?（何名様ですか。）

Unit 2 受診

Dialogue
A = Receptionist B = Patient

Audio 1-10

In the waiting room
A: Good morning. May I help you?
B: Good morning, I'm Richard Cook. I have an appointment for 11:30.
A: Let me see. Yes, we have you right here, Mr. Cook.
B: That's good.
A: ① May I see your medical insurance card, please?
B: Yes, here you are.
A: Let me check. Okay. ② Could you fill out this form? Then please answer the questions about your medical history by circling 'yes' or 'no.'
B: Sure, no problem.

A few minutes later
B: Here you go.
A: Thank you, Mr. Cook. Please have a seat and wait until I call you.
B: Okay, thanks.

Ten minutes later
A: Mr. Cook. Here is your new ID card for this clinic. Please use it whenever you come here.
B: Right, I will.
A: Next. Please follow the signs to counter Number 5 and hand this file

to the nurse there. Do you have any questions?

B: Yes. Where is counter number 5?

A: Follow the green arrows to the end of this hall and then turn right. You can't miss it.

B: Okay, thank you.

Vocabulary Check　Audio 1-11

(1)〜(10)に合う語義をそれぞれ (a)〜(j) から選びなさい。

(1) arrow　　　(　)　　(2) circle　　　　　(　)
(3) counter　　(　)　　(4) fill out　　　　(　)
(5) follow　　 (　)　　(6) hand　　　　　　(　)
(7) have a seat (　)　　(8) medical history (　)
(9) miss　　　 (　)　　(10) sign　　　　　　(　)

(a) 病歴　　(b) 標示　　(c) 窓口　　(d) 矢印　　(e) 座る　　(f) 手渡す
(g) 〜に従って進む　(h) 見落とす　(i) 必要事項を記入する　(j) 〜を丸で囲む

許可を求める表現　Audio 1-12

Dialogue 中の下線部①の表現を参考にし、音声を聴いて（　　）を埋めましょう。

(1)「これを試着してもいいですか。」「ええ、いいですよ。」
 "(　　)(　　)(　　) this (　　)?" "Sure."

(2)「あなたの辞書を借りてもいいですか。」「いいですよ。どうぞ。」
 "(　　)(　　)(　　) your dictionary?" "Of course. Here you are."

(3)「メニューを見せていただけませんか。」「かしこまりました。すぐにお持ちします。」
 "(　　)(　　)(　　) the menu?" "Certainly. I'll bring it right away."

(4)「ここでタバコを吸ってもいいですか。」「すみませんが、控えてください。」
 "Would you (　　)(　　)(　　)(　　) here?" "I'm sorry, but I do."

(5)「約束をキャンセルしてもよろしいでしょうか。」「いいですよ。でもなぜですか。」
 "Would it (　　)(　　)(　　)(　　)(　　) cancel my appointment?" "Yes, but why?"

(6)「このパソコンを使ってもよろしいでしょうか。」「はい、どうぞ。」
 "(　　)(　　) okay (　　)(　　) use this computer?" "Sure, go ahead."

依頼の表現

Audio 1-13

Dialogue 中の下線部②の表現を参考にし、音声を聴いて（　　）を埋めましょう。

(1) "(　　)(　　)(　　) your seat."
"Oh, thank you."
(「どうぞそのまま座ったままでいてください。」「ありがとうございます。」)

(2) "(　　)(　　)(　　)(　　) the salt, please?"
"Sure, here you are."
(「塩を取ってくれませんか。」「はいどうぞ。」)

(3) "Excuse me, but (　　)(　　)(　　)(　　) again?"
"Of course."
(「もう一度繰り返してくれませんか。」「いいですよ。」)

(4) "(　　)(　　)(　　) carry my luggage to the room?"
"Certainly, ma'am."
(「部屋まで私の荷物を運んでいただけませんか。」「かしこまりました。」)

(5) "(　　)(　　)(　　)(　　)(　　) this work, please?"
"Sorry... I wish (　　)(　　), but I have to leave now."
(「この仕事を手伝ってくれませんか。」「ごめんなさい。できればそうしたいのですが、もう帰らないといけないんです。」)

(6) "Would you (　　)(　　) this table?"
"Not at all."
(「このテーブルを片付けてくれませんか。」「いいですよ。」)

(7) "I was (　　)(　　)(　　)(　　) make copies of this document for me."
"Okay. How many?"
(「この書類をコピーしていただけないでしょうか。」「分かりました。何枚必要ですか。」)

(8) "I'd (　　) it if you could (　　)(　　) some advice about this."
"Sure, (　　)(　　)(　　)(　　)."
(「このことについて助言をいただきたいのですが。」「ええ、喜んで。」)

(9) "Would it be (　　)(　　)(　　) to my office around 2:00 p.m.?"
"No problem."
(「2時頃、私のオフィスに来ていただけないでしょうか。」「いいですよ。」)

Everyday Conversation

At the Bluebird Restaurant

🔊 Audio 1-14

A = Waiter   B = Ken   C = Jane

A: Good evening. Welcome to the Bluebird Restaurant! How may I help you?
B: Yes, I have a reservation for this evening.
A: May I ask your name, please?
B: Yes, It's Nakamura.
A: Let me see…. Ah, yes, here you are. Thank you, Mr. Nakamura. I'll show you to your table.
B: Thank you.

They finish taking their seats.

A: ① <u>Here is the menu and wine list.</u> Would you care for a drink?
B: Yes, I'll have a draft beer, please.
C: I'd like a glass of white wine.
A: All right. I'll bring them right away.

A few minutes later

A: ② <u>Here is your beer, and this is your wine.</u> May I take your order now?
B: Actually we are still deciding. Could you give us a few more minutes?
A: Of course.

Five minutes later

A: So, have you decided?
B: Yes, we have. Thanks. I'll have the sirloin steak.
A: How would you like your steak done?
B: Medium, please.
A: All right. How about the potatoes?
B: A baked potato with sour cream and chives, please.
A: Excellent. And how about you, ma'am?
C: I'd like to have the avocado salmon salad to start, and then the roast beef dinner.
A: Perfect. How about dessert?
B: Not for me, thank you. I'll have a coffee after dinner instead.
C: Could I have the ice cream with chocolate sauce and a cappuccino?
A: Excellent. I'll be back in a few minutes with your food.

After their meal

A: ③<u>How was your meal?</u>
B: Fantastic!
C: Yeah, the food was great and the atmosphere was also wonderful.
A: Thank you very much. ④<u>Here's your bill.</u>
B: Do you accept credit cards?
A: Yes, of course.
B: Please add a 15% tip to the bill.
A: Yes, sir. Thank you very much.
B: It's my treat tonight.
C: Hey, just a second.
B: No, no, no. Tonight's dinner is on me. I've been wanting to talk with you for a long time.
C: Thank you, Ken. ⑤<u>I'm happy we finally had a chance to talk over a nice dinner.</u>

※ to start「まず始めに」 instead「代わりに」 tip「チップ」 bill「勘定」

相手に物を差し出す時の表現

Audio 1-15

Dialogue 中の下線部①②④の表現を参照し、音声を聴いて、リピートしましょう。

(1) Here is your ticket.（こちらはお客様のチケットです。）

(2) Here are your passport and boarding pass.
（こちらはお客様のパスポートと搭乗券です。）

相手に感想を尋ねる表現

Dialogue 中の下線部③の表現を使い、(　　)を埋めましょう。

(1)「映画はどうだった？」「期待していた以上に面白かったよ。」
"How was the movie?" "It was (　　) (　　) (　　) (　　) I had expected."

(2)「昨夜のサッカーの試合どうでしたか？」「わくわくしました」
"How was the soccer game?" "It was (　　)."

(3)「彼の演説はいかがでしたか。」「とてもつまらないものでした。」
"How was his speech?" "It was really (　　)."

(4)「ディナーはいかがでしたか。」「とてもおいしかったです。」
"How (　　) (　　) (　　　) the dinner?" "It was really good."

「〜しながら話す」という表現　　　🔊 Audio 1-16

Dialogue 中の下線部⑤の表現を参照し、音声を聴いて、リピートしましょう。

★ over は、talk や discuss など「話す」という動詞と共に用いて、「〜しながら話す」という意味で使われます。

(1) Shall we talk over a cup of coffee?（コーヒーでも飲みながら話さない？）

(2) We chatted over a glass of wine.（私たちはワインを飲みながらおしゃべりをしました。）

(3) Let's discuss this over lunch.（この件に関しては食事をしながら話し合いましょう。）

Useful Expressions　　　🔊 Audio 1-17

音声を聴いて、(　　) を埋めましょう。

(1)「何名様でしょうか。」「3名です。」
"(　　) (　　) (　　　), sir?"
"Three people."

(2)「ご注文はお決まりですか。」「いいえ、まだです。もう少し待っていただけますか。」
"(　　) (　　) (　　) (　　) (　　)?"
"No, I haven't decided (　　). Give us a few minutes?"

(3)「何がお勧めですか。」「本日のお勧めはタラのグリルレモンソース添えです。」
"What would you (　　)?"
"Today's (　　) is Grilled Codfish with lemon sauce."

(4)「ランチには飲み物は含まれていますか。」「いいえ、含まれていません。」
"Does the lunch special (　　) (　　) (　　)?"
"I'm afraid not."

(5)「すみませんが、私の注文した料理がまだ来ていません。」「申し訳ございません。すぐにお持ちします。」
"Excuse me, my (　　) (　　) (　　) yet."
"Sorry, sir. I'll bring it right away."

(6)「そろそろ出ようか。」「そうだね。お勘定をお願いしよう。すみません！」
"It's about time to leave."
"Yeah. Let's (　　) (　　) (　　) (　　). Excuse me, waiter?"

(7)「すみません、お勘定をお願いします。」「かしこまりました。少々お待ちを。すぐにお持ちします。」

"Excuse me, could we (　　　) (　　　) (　　　), please?"

"Certainly. Just a moment, I'll be right back."

(8)「すみません。このレシートに間違いがあるようです。私達、ワインを頼んでいません。」

"Excuse me. There seems to be (　　　) (　　　) (　　　) this receipt. We didn't order any wine."

Registration Form for Outpatients

Date	Year	/ Month	/ Day
Name	First Name		Last Name

Sex		Date of Birth		Age	
Address					Zip Code
Nationality			Phone #		
Occupation					
Name of Work Place					
Address of Work Place					
Phone # of Work Place					
Insurance					

Department

(✓) Internal Medicine	( ) Surgery	( ) Orthopedics
( ) Pediatrics	( ) Dermatology	( ) ENT
( ) Ophthalmology	( ) Obstetrics & Gynecology	( ) Urology
( ) Psychiatry	( ) Pain Management	( ) Neurosurgery
( ) Dentistry	( ) Physical Therapy	( ) Other

Medical Questionnaire

Date: Apr. 22nd, 2015

Name:	First name / Middle name / Last name	Sex	
	Richard Cook	M (✓)	F ( )
	Date of Birth: Year / Month / Day	Age	Blood Type
	1971 / 4 / 21	43	O

Temperature	Blood Pressure	
36.5℃	/	mmHg

Height	177 cm	Weight	72 kg

1-(1)	What symptoms do you have today?		
	I have been suffering from stomachache.		
1-(2)	When did you first notice this pain?		
	A week ago.		
2	Tell us about your medical history.		
	I had my appendix removed.	At the age of (	15)
		At the age of (	)
3-(1)	Are you taking any medicines now?	Yes ( )	No (✓)
3-(2)	If you answered yes above, tell us what kind of medicine you are taking.	Yes ( )	
3-(3)	Have you ever had an allergy to medication?	Yes ( )	No (✓)
4-(1)	Are you taking any medication at the moment?	Yes ( )	No (✓)
4-(2)	If you answered yes above, tell us about it.		
5	Are you allergic to any food?	Yes ( )	No (✓)
6-(1)	Do you smoke?	Yes ( )	No (✓)
6-(2)	If you answered yes above, tell me how much you smoke?		/ day
7-(1)	Do you drink alcohol?	Yes (✓)	No ( )
7-(2)	If you answered yes above, how often you drink?	sometimes	
8	Are you pregnant?	Yes ( )	No ( )

Unit 3 問診・医師による診察

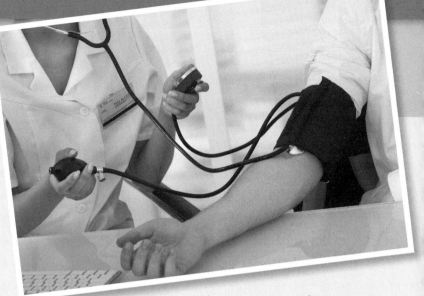

 **Dialogue**

A = Nurse B = Patient

Audio 1-18

In the examining room

A: First of all, ①I'd like to take your temperature. Please put this under your arm.

B: All right.

A minute later

A: Okay, let's see. It is 36.5 degrees Celsius. Perfect. Next, ②I'd like to check your blood pressure. Please roll up your sleeve.

B: Okay.

A: Excellent. Your blood pressure is normal. Now, ③I'd like to ask you a few questions. ④How have you been feeling? ⑤Have you noticed any symptoms in particular?

B: I have a stomachache constantly.

A: I see. What kind of pain do you have?

B: A sharp pain.

A: When did you first notice it?

B: About a week ago.

A: Okay, thank you, Mr. Cook. Dr. Clifford will see you soon. Please wait here for a few minutes.

Vocabulary Check　　Audio 1-19

(1)～(8) に合う語義をそれぞれ (a)～(h) から選びなさい。

(1) blood pressure (　)　　(2) degree (　)
(3) in particular (　)　　(4) normal (　)
(5) notice (　)　　(6) sleeve (　)
(7) symptom (　)　　(8) temperature (　)

(a) 血圧　　(b) 袖　　(c) 症状　　(d) 体温　　(e) 度　　(f) 正常な
(g) 特に　　(h) 気付く

※ Fahrenheit「華氏」から Celsius「摂氏」への換算式：$C = (F - 32) \times 5 \div 9$

Useful Expressions

❶ Dialogue 中の下線部①～③を発音練習しましょう。
❷ 音声を聴いて、リピートしましょう。　　Audio 1-20

◇ I want ~. I would like ~.（～がほしい）
　"What do you want?" "I want a glass of orange juice."
　"Would you like a drink?" "Thank you. I'd like a cup of tea."

◇ I want to do ~. I would like to do ~.（～したい）
　I want to go to the movies this afternoon.
　I'd like to eat out tonight.

◇ I want O to do ~. I would like O to do ~.（O に～してもらいたい）
　I want you to join me at the concert tonight.
　I'd like you to explain about the pain.

❸ (1)～(3) は＜　＞内の語を並べ替えて、英文を完成させましょう。ただし、文頭に来る語も小文字で示しています。また (4) の英文を完成させましょう。

(1) オフィスの近くのあのイタリア料理の店に行きたいです。
　<the / like / office / to / near / Italian / I'd / our / go / restaurant / to>.

_____

(2) ラジオを消しましょうか。
　<radio / want / off / do / to / the / me / you / turn>?

_____

(3) 駅まであなたを迎えに行きましょうか。
<at / would / pick / station / you / me / you / to / up / the / like>?

_____

(4) 将来は看護師になりたいですか？

_____

❹ Dialogue 中の下線部④現在完了進行形と⑤現在完了形を参照し、(　　　　)に適切な語を書きましょう。

◇現在完了形 S + have[has] +過去分詞形
◇現在完了進行形 S + have[has] been ～ing.

(1) 私は 1997 年からハワイで暮らしています。
　　I have (　　　) in Hawaii (　　　) 1997.

(2) 当機はただいま成田国際空港に到着しました。
　　We (　　　) just (　　　) at Narita International Airport.

(3) これまでカナダに行ったことはありますか？―いいえ、まだ行ったことはありません。
　　(　　　) you ever (　　　) (　　　) Canada? – No, I (　　　) yet.

(4) ずいぶん久しぶりですね。お元気でいらっしゃいましたか？
　　It (　　　) been a long time! How (　　　) you (　　　)?

(5) これまで薬にアレルギー反応はありましたか？
　　(　　　) you ever (　　　) an (　　　) (　　　) medication?

(6) 私は一度も呼吸困難になったことはありません。
　　I (　　　) (　　　) had any difficulty in (　　　).

(7) 私は風邪を引いてしまいました。
　　I (　　　) (　　　) a cold.

(8) 私の娘が喘息にかかってしまいました。
　　My daughter (　　　) (　　　) asthma.

(9) 彼はずっと高血圧症に罹っています。
　　He (　　　) (　　　) (　　　) from high blood pressure.

(10) 私は 10 年間ずっとここで看護師として働いています。
　　I have (　　　) (　　　) here as a nurse (　　　) ten years.

 **Dialogue**

A = Doctor   B = Patient

Audio 1-21

In the doctor's office

A: Mr. Cook. Please come in.

Mr. Cook enters the room.

A: I'm Dr. Clifford. Nice to meet you, Mr. Cook. Please have a seat here.

B: Thank you.

A: ①This chart says you have had a stomachache for a week.

B: Yes, it's been getting worse.

A: When do you feel the pain?

B: I feel it constantly, but especially after meals.

A: Are you sleeping well?

B: No, sometimes I can't sleep because of the pain.

A: ②That sounds tough. How's your appetite?

B: Not good. Actually I've lost weight lately.

A: Have you ever had a stomach ulcer before?

B: No, this is the first time for me to feel like this.

A: I see. Have you ever had a stomach examination such as a gastroscopy?

B: No, I haven't.

A: I see. … Right, please open your mouth and say "Ahhhh."

B: Ahhhhh…

A: I'm going to feel your neck. … Good. And now I'm going to listen to your heart. Take a deep breath in and out. … Okay, it sounds fine. Now, I'm going to examine your stomach. Could you lie down on this bed?

B: Sure.

A: I'm going to gently press on your stomach. Please tell me if you feel any pain.

B: Okay…ah, there. It hurts there where you just touched me.

A: Okay. Please sit up. I'm going to prescribe some medicine, so please take it for a week. ③However, if the pain still persists, you'll need to have a further examination, so please come and see me again.

B: Right. Thank you.

A: Please take care.

Vocabulary Check　　Audio 1-22

(1) ～ (8) に合う語義をそれぞれ (a) ～ (h) から選びなさい。

(1) actually　　(　)　　(2) appetite　　(　)
(3) examination　(　)　　(4) gently　　(　)
(5) lately　　(　)　　(6) lose weight　(　)
(7) prescribe　(　)　　(8) work overtime　(　)

(a) 検査　(b) 食欲　(c) 最近　(d) 実は　(e) 優しく　(f) 残業する
(g) 処方する　(h) 体重が減る

Useful Expressions　　Audio 1-23

❶ Dialogue 中の下線部①を参照し、音声を聴いて、(　) を埋めましょう。

(1) この記事には癌の新しい治療法が発見されたと書かれています。
　This (　) (　) a new (　) for cancer has been developed.

(2) 今日の新聞によると、昨日商店街で大火事が発生したということです。
　Today's (　) (　) there was a big (　) in a shopping arcade yesterday.

(3) 天気予報では、今日の午後は雨になるそうです。
　The (　) forecast (　) it's going to be rainy (　) afternoon.

(4) 時計は今1時45分を指しています。
　The (　) (　) (　) 1:45.

(5) そのラベルにはそれが日本製だと書かれています。
　The (　) (　) it's made (　) Japan.

(6) その看板には「遊泳禁止」と書かれています。
　That (　) (　) "No Swimming Here."

❷ Dialogue 中の下線部②を参照し、音声を聴いて、リピートしましょう。　　Audio 1-24

★相手が言ったことを that で受けて「それは～のようですね」と応える表現です。この that は省略されることもあります。

(1) "How about going to the amusement park tomorrow?"
　"That sounds exciting!"

(2) "I'm going to a jazz concert tonight."　"Sounds nice."

(3) "Why don't we go to the movies after school?"　"Sounds good."

❸ Dialogue 中の下線部③を参照し、(　　)内を埋めなさい。

★時や条件を表す副詞節の中では、未来のことは現在形で表します。

(1) もし明日雨になれば、コンサートは延期されます。
    If it (　　　) tomorrow, the concert (　　　) (　　　) postponed.

(2) もし今夜時間があれば、彼女は私たちとの夕食に参加するでしょう。
    If she (　　　) time tonight, she (　　　) (　　　) us for dinner.

活動の場を日本から海外へ広げていくきっかけとなったのは…

　中学生の頃、インドの写真集を見ました。川で水浴びをする人、路上で寝ている人、物乞いをしている人。これらの写真を見たとき、発作的に「この国に行って働きたい」と思いました。可哀想な人々を助けたいという思いよりも、異文化の世界で働きたいという好奇心でわくわくしたのです。私はラジオで英語の勉強を始めました。助産師学校の時、クラスメートがアフリカで開発事業を行っている日本企業が助産師を探していると教えてくれました。私はすぐに応募し、日本での臨床経験10か月でコンゴ民主共和国に派遣されました。看護師・助産師として経験が浅く未熟な私を現地の人はとても優しく見守り励ましてくれ、そのことがアフリカにのめり込んでゆくきっかけとなりました。

Unit 4 薬の服用

Dialogue

A = Nurse   B = Patient   C = Pharmacist

Audio 1-25

A: Mr. Cook, here is the prescription for your medication. Could you please take it to the pharmacy?
B: Okay. Is the pharmacy on the first floor close to the main entrance?
A: Yes, that's right.
B: Thank you.

At the pharmacy

C: Mr. Cook, here are your medications. ①<u>There are five different medicines.</u> You will need to take each medicine every day for a week.
B: Okay, I see. Are there any special instructions?
C: Yes, there are. ②<u>Please be careful to follow the directions appropriately.</u>
B: Could you please explain the instructions for each medicine?
C: Yes, of course. ③<u>I was just about to do that.</u> You have white tablets, capsules, a liquid medicine, a powder, and suppositories.
B: That is a lot of medicine! Do I really need them all?
C: Yes, unfortunately you do. The tablets will ease your pain. Please take one tablet three times a day after each meal. Please take the powder at the same time. It will settle your stomach.
B: Okay, how about the capsules?
C: This is an antibiotic. It reduces any inflammation. Please take one once a day before breakfast.

B: Alright. And what about the last two?
C: Well, use the small cup provided, please take 50 ml of the liquid medicine twice a day: Once before breakfast, and again once before dinner. It helps with digestion. ④Also, please remember to shake it well before taking any.
B: I see. And this last one?
C: This is a suppository. It must be taken if the pain gets really bad. Please be careful as it is not like the other medicines. It needs to be administered via the anus.
B: Okay. I understand.
C: Oh, one final thing. ⑤Please remember to keep the liquid medicine and suppositories in your fridge. They need to stay cold.
B: Okay, I think I've got it — five different types of medications.
C: Excellent. If you have any other questions or concerns, please consult your doctor or pharmacist.
B: I will. Thank you.
C: Please take good care of yourself.

※ provided「備え付けの、付属の」 administer「薬を投与する」

Warm-up

薬の種類について、(1)〜(6)の薬の名前を(a)〜(f)から選びなさい。

(1) antibiotics　　　(　)　　(2) capsule　　　　(　)
(3) liquid medicine (　)　　(4) powder　　　　(　)
(5) suppository　　 (　)　　(6) tablet　　　　 (　)

(a) 錠剤　　(b) カプセル　　(c) 抗生物質　　(d) 粉薬　　(e) 座薬　　(f) 水薬

Vocabulary Check

(1)～(14) に合う語義を (a)～(n) から選びなさい。

(1) anus   (　)　　(2) appropriately (　)
(3) consult   (　)　　(4) digestion   (　)
(5) directions   (　)　　(6) follow   (　)
(7) fridge (=refrigerator) (　)　(8) inflammation (　)
(9) meal   (　)　　(10) pharmacist   (　)
(11) pharmacy   (　)　　(12) prescription (　)
(13) reduce   (　)　　(14) settle   (　)

(a) 説明書、使用法　(b) 肛門　(c) 冷蔵庫　(d) 薬局　(e) 薬剤師　(f) 処方箋
(g) 炎症　(h) 消化　(i) 食事　(j) 鎮める　(k) 従う　(l) 相談する
(m) 弱める　(n) 正しく、適切に

Useful Expressions

❶ Dialogue 中の下線部①を参照し、(　) に適切な be 動詞を書きなさい。時制にも注意しましょう。

There is ~. ／ There are ~. ／ There was ~. ／ There were ~. ／ There will be ~.
を使って、「～がある」という表現の練習をしましょう。

(1) There (　　) a big shopping mall near the station.
（駅の近くに大型ショッピングセンターがあります。）

(2) There (　　) many shoppers at the mall every weekend.
（そのショッピングセンターには、週末になるとたくさんの買い物客でいっぱいです。）

(3) There (　　) five people in our family.（私の家族は5人家族です。）

(4) There (　　) a phone call for you.（あなたに電話がかかってきています。）

(5) There (　　) no water in the shower.（シャワーから水が出ません。）

(6) There (　　) a lot of money in the safe.（金庫の中に大金が入っています。）

(7) There (　　) a lot of useful information on this web site.
（このサイトにはたくさんの役立つ情報があります。）

(8) There (　　) a concert last Sunday.（先週の土曜日にコンサートがありました。）

(9) There (　　) about five thousand fans in the concert hall.
（コンサートホールにはおよそ5千人のファンが集まりました。）

(10) There (　　) some mistakes in my paper.
（私の論文にはいくつか間違いがありました。）

(11) There (   ) enough food and beer on the tables.
　　（テーブルには十分な量の食べ物とビールがありました。）

(12) There (   ) (   ) a special exhibit in this museum next month.
　　（来月この博物館で特別展示があります。）

❷ Dialogue 中の下線部②を参照し、音声を聴いて、(　　)を埋めましょう。　　Audio 1-27

(1) 風邪を引かないように注意してください。
　　Please be careful not to (   ) (   ) (   ).

(2) 階段から滑り落ちないように気を付けてください。
　　Please be careful not to (   ) (   ) the stairs.

❸ Dialogue 中の下線部③を参照し、音声を聴いて、リピートしましょう。

(1) 携帯電話が鳴った時、ちょうど家を出ようとしていたんです。
　　When my cell phone rang, I was just about to leave home.

(2) ああ、フィリップス先生！ちょうど先生をお呼びしようとしていたところでした。
　　Oh, Dr. Philips! I was just about to call for you.

❹ Dialogue 中の下線部④⑤を参照し、音声を聴いて、(　　)を埋めましょう。

(1) 手洗いとうがいを忘れないようにしてください。
　　Please remember to (   ) your (   ) and (   ) well.

(2) 薬を服用中は、アルコールを飲まないようにしてください。
　　Please remember (   ) (   ) drink (   ) while you are taking any medicine.

薬の説明

(1) 〜 (4) は (a) 〜 (d) の薬について説明したものです。答えを [　] に書きなさい。

(1) [　] You should take this tablet in order to relieve pain and to reduce fever and inflammation.

(2) [　] You should take this tablet for sore throats.

(3) [　] You should use this device to administer the drug to relieve asthma.

(4) [　] You should rub this on your skin when you feel itchy.

　　(a) aspirin　　(b) inhaler　　(c) lozenge　　(d) ointment

Unit 4

薬の服用

Unit 4　薬についての表現　　Audio 1-28

❶音声を聴いて、リピートしましょう。

(1) Please take this pill before you go to bed.（就寝前にこの薬を服用して下さい。）

(2) Don't take an excessive amount of sleeping pills.
（睡眠薬を多量に服用してはいけません。）

(3) The patient overdosed on aspirin.（その患者はアスピリンを過剰摂取した。）

(4) Please follow the directions on the label.（ラベルの指示に従ってください。）

(5) Do not breast-feed while taking this medication.
（この薬を服用しているときは、授乳をやめてください。）

(6) Take this medicine with water.（この薬は水と一緒に服用して下さい。）

(7) Do not chew this medicine.（この薬は噛まずに服用して下さい。）

(8) Please use this inhaler when you have asthma.
（喘息の症状が出たら、この吸入器を使用してください。）

(9) Could you fill this prescription for me?（この処方箋の薬を調合していただけますか。）

(10) My doctor prescribed some pills for my headache.
（先生が私の頭痛に丸薬を処方してくれました。）

❷音声を聴いて、（　　）に適切な語を書きなさい。　　Audio 1-29

(1) 痒いときに、この軟膏を擦り込んでください。
When you (　　) (　　), apply this ointment.

(2) この薬は眠気を引き起こす可能性があるので、運転や大型機械の操作をしないでください。
Because this medicine can make you feel (　　), do not drive or (　　) heavy machinery.

(3) 何か異変を感じたら、薬の服用をやめてください。
(　　) (　　) these medicines if you feel something is (　　).

(4) 妊娠している場合には、医師または薬剤師に相談してください。
(　　) your doctor or pharmacist if you are (　　).

(5) 子供の手の届くところに保管しないでください。
Keep the medicine (　　) (　　) children's (　　).

(6) コンタクトレンズを装着したままで点眼してもいいです。
You may apply (　　) (　　) when you are (　　) contact lenses.

(7) この薬は痰を取り除きます。
This capsule (　　) phlegm.

(8) これまで薬物アレルギーが出たことはありますか。
Have you ever had a (　　) (　　)?

(9) この薬は副作用がほとんどありません。
This drug has few (　　) (　　).

Unit 5 再受診・検査

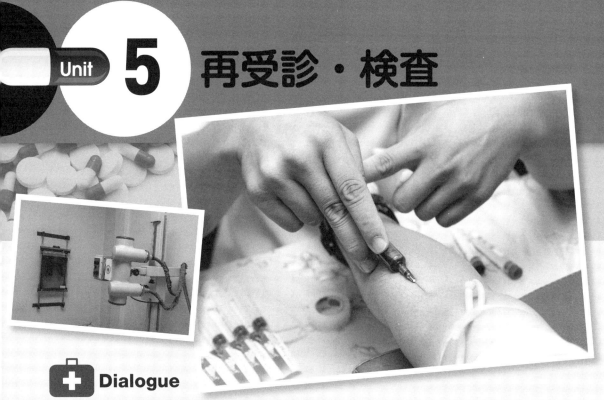

Dialogue

A = Doctor   B = Patient   C = Nurse   D = Radiologist

Audio 1-30

In the doctor's office
A: Good morning, Mr. Cook. How have you been?
B: ①Actually I still have a sharp pain in my stomach. ②The pain has been getting worse. And I vomited yesterday and I've been feeling nauseous.
A: Oh, I see. Did you take your medicine for the past week?
B: Yes, I did. But I stayed home yesterday because of it.
A: I see. Mr. Cook, did you have breakfast this morning?
B: No, I didn't.
A: Okay. Well, let's begin with a blood test. And then, we'll take an X-ray of your stomach. Please follow the nurse's instructions. When you've finished these, please come back here and we'll discuss your results.
B: Okay. Thank you.

In the treatment room
C: Okay, it's time for your blood test. Please roll up your right sleeve.
B: All right.
C: This may hurt a little, but try to relax.

After the blood has been taken
C: There we go. Now I'll put a band aid on you and we'll be finished here.

B: Thank you.
C: Next, we'll take an abdominal X-ray. ③Do you know where the X-ray room is?
B: No, I don't. ④Could you show me, please?
C: Sure. ⑤Take the elevator to the second floor. When you get out of the elevator, turn right. ⑥Then go straight ahead, and you'll find the X-ray room on your left.
B: Thank you.

In the X-ray room

D: May I see your file, please?
B: Here you are.
D: Okay, Mr. Cook. Please come in. Could you change into this robe, please?
B: Sure.

※ turn right「右折する」 x-ray room「レントゲン室」 come in「中に入る」 take off「脱ぐ」 put on「着る」

Vocabulary Check   Audio 1-31

(1)〜(6) に合う語義をそれぞれ (a)〜(f) から選びなさい。

(1) discuss   (   )   (2) examine   (   )
(3) nauseous   (   )   (4) result   (   )
(5) sleeve   (   )   (6) vomit   (   )

(a) 検査結果　(b) 気分が悪い　(c) 袖　(d) 検査する　(e) 吐く　(f) 話し合う

痛みについての表現   Audio 1-32

Dialogue 中の下線部①を参照し、音声を聴いて、リピートしましょう。

(1) Where does it hurt? ／ Where is your pain?（どこが痛みますか？）

(2) My stomach hurts.（胃が痛みます。）

(3) Does it hurt much?（とても痛みますか？）

(4) I feel the pain especially when I'm hungry.（特に空腹時に痛みます。）

(5) I have a griping pain in the stomach.（お腹がきりきり痛みます。）

(6) I sometimes feel pain in my chest.（時々胸に痛みを感じます。）

(7) The pain has become severe.（痛みがひどくなってきました。）

(8) I have a throbbing headache.（頭がズキズキ痛みます。）

(9) My back badly aches.（腰がとてもひどく痛みます。）

(10) I feel sore all over because of that hard exercise.
（あんなに激しく運動したから、体中があちこち痛みます。）

比較の表現 Audio 1-33

Dialogue 中の下線部②を参照し、音声を聴いて、（　）に適切な語を入れなさい。

(1) 思っていたより痛かった。
It hurt (　　　　) than I expected.

(2) 昨日よりも痛みがひどいです。
The pain is (　　　　) now than it was yesterday.

(3) 彼女は快方に向かっています。
She is getting (　　　　).

(4) この医学書はそれよりも難しい。
This medical book is (　　　　) (　　　　) than that.

(5) 彼女の病気は当初私たちが考えたよりも深刻だった。
Her illness was (　　　　) (　　　　) than we first thought.

(6) 試験に合格するために、もっと勉強しなくちゃね。
We should study (　　　　) to pass the examination.

間接疑問文の語順の確認

Dialogue 中の下線部③を参照し、英作文に挑戦しましょう。疑問詞の後は平叙文の語順 (S+V) になります。

(1) How long will it take for the wound to heal?
I wonder _____

(2) Where is the pharmacy?
Could you tell me _____

(3) How far is it to the medical center?
Do you know _____

(4) When did the pain start?
Can you tell me _____

(5) Where does it hurt?
Tell me _____

道を尋ねる表現　　Audio 1-34

Dialogue 中の下線部④を参照し、音声を聴いて、（　）を埋めましょう。

(1) 駅までの行き方を教えていただけませんか。
Could you (　　) (　　) (　　) (　　) (　　) the station, please?

(2) この歯科医院にはどうやって行くのですか？
(　　) (　　) (　　) (　　) (　　) this dental office?

(3) 眼科診療所の場所が分かりません。行き方を教えてくれませんか。
I don't know where the eye clinic is. Could you please (　　) (　　) (　　)?

take を使った「乗り物などを利用する」表現　　Audio 1-35

Dialogue 中の下線部⑤を参照し、音声を聴いて、リピートしましょう。

(1) You should take an escalator to the third floor.
（3階までエスカレーターで行った方がいいですよ。）

(2) I think we should take the subway to the station.
（駅まで地下鉄で行った方がよさそうだね。）

(3) Shall we take a taxi to the hospital?（病院までタクシーで行きましょう。）

(4) I always try to take the stairs instead of the elevator in order to get more exercise.
（運動のために、私はエレベーターではなく、階段を利用するようにしています。）

道案内をする時の表現　　Audio 1-36

Dialogue 中の下線部⑥を参照し、音声を聴いて、（　）を埋めましょう。

(1) 次の角で左に曲がってください。それは薬局の隣にありますよ。
Turn left at the next corner and it is (　　) (　　) the pharmacy.

(2) 3つ目の角で右に曲がってください。そうすればレストランは右側にありますよ。
Take the third right and the restaurant is (　　) your right.

(3) それは本屋と郵便局の間にあります。
It's (　　) the book shop (　　) the post office.

(4) それはコンビニの向かい側にありますよ。
It's (　　) the convenience store.

(5) 左手に診療所が見えてきます。
(　　) (　　) the clinic on your left.

Everyday Conversation

At the Airport Lobby

Audio 1-37

A = Receptionist at the information desk   B = Passenger

A: Good afternoon, what can I do for you?
B: Excuse me, but I'd like to go to Grand Hotel downtown. How can I get there?
A: Well, you can get there by subway, shuttle bus or taxi. The shuttle bus has just left, and the next one will come in an hour. Hmm, you have a lot of baggage, so I think you should take a taxi.
B: I see. ① How long does it take to get to the hotel by taxi?
A: I think it will take about 20 minutes.
B: Good. Do you know how much the fare is?
A: ② I'm not sure exactly, but it'll cost about $30. You should ask the driver.
B: Okay, thanks. Could you tell me where the taxi stand is?
A: Sure. Go up this hallway, and turn left. Then take the elevator to the first floor. You can find a taxi stand right outside the exit.
B: Thank you very much.
A: You're welcome.

Vocabulary Check

Audio 1-38

(1) 〜 (4) に合う語義をそれぞれ (a) 〜 (d) から選びなさい。

(1) cost   (　)   (2) exit   (　)
(3) fare   (　)   (4) taxi stand   (　)

(a) 運賃   (b) タクシー乗り場   (c) 出口   (d) 費用がかかる

Useful Expressions

Audio 1-39

❶ Dialogue 中の下線部①を参照し、音声を聴いて、(　) を埋めましょう。

(1)「宿題を終わらせるのにどれくらいかかりそう？」「たぶん1時間ぐらいかかると思う。」
"How long (　　) (　　) (　　) to finish doing your homework?"
"I think (　　) (　　) about (　　) (　　)."

(2)「すっかり元気になるのにどれくらいかかったの？」「約1カ月かかりました。」
"How long (　　)(　　)(　　)(　　) recover completely?"
"(　　)(　　)(　　) about a month."

❷ Dialogue 中の下線部②を参照し、音声を聴いて、(　　)を埋めましょう。

(1)「それはいくらですか？」「58ドル25セントです。」
"How much (　　) it cost?" "(　　)(　　) $58.25."

(2)「その新しい靴、高かったんでしょうね！いくらしたの。」「たったの30ドルよ。本当にお買い得でした。」
"Those new shoes must have been expensive! How much (　　)(　　)(　　)?"
"They cost only $30. They were a great bargain."

道案内をする　　🔊 Audio 1-40

❶ペアになって練習してみましょう。

A: Excuse me, but I'm lost. Could you tell me the way to the convention center?

B: Sure. It's not so far. Go straight for two blocks and then take a left. The convention center will be on your right. You can't miss it!

A: Oh, thank you. It's nice of you.

B: My pleasure.

※ be lost「道に迷っている」　take a left「左折する」　miss「見逃す」　My pleasure.「どういたしまして。」

❷ペアになって練習してみましょう。

A: Excuse me, would you mind showing me the way to the national museum?

B: Not at all. (*Pointing at the map*) We are here on this map. Go straight along this street for three blocks and turn right. And then walk for one block and then make a left at the first traffic light. The museum is between the office buildings.

A: Thank you very much.

B: No problem.

※ block「区画」　make a left「左折する」　traffic light「信号機」

Unit 6 胃の検査

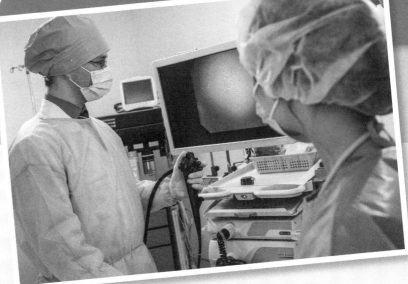

Dialogue

A = Doctor   B = Patient

🔊 Audio 1-41

In the doctor's office

A: Mr. Cook, from the results of today's examination, I think we need to do a few more tests.

B: Oh, is there anything serious?

A: I don't know for sure, but just to be safe, I would like to take a look inside your stomach with a gastroscope.

B: Oh, okay. I see.

A: Would it be possible to come tomorrow morning for a gastroscopy exam?

B: Okay.

A: Good. ① <u>Then please be here by 9:00 a.m.</u> Remember not to eat anything after 9:00 p.m. tonight. ② <u>But you may drink water until 10:00 p.m.</u> Your nurse will explain the procedure. Please ask her if you have any questions.

B: Thank you.

A. You're welcome. See you then.

※ precise examination「精密検査」 gastroscope「胃カメラ」 procedure「手順、手続き」

by / until を使った表現

❶ Dialogue 中の下線部①を参照し、音声を聴いて、リピートしましょう。　　　Audio 1-42

(1) Please be at gate 7 by 3:00 p.m.（3時までに7番ゲートにお越しください。）

(2) She'll be here in time for the meeting.（彼女は会議に間に合うように来ます。）

(3) I'm Lisa Clifford. I'm here for my two o'clock interview today.
（リサ・クリフォードと申します。2時からの面接で伺いました。）

(4) "Hello, Lisa. Where are you?" "Hi, Steve. I'm almost there."
（「もしもし、リサ。今どこにいるの？」「スティーヴ、もうすぐ着くから。」）

❷ Dialogue 中の下線部②を参照し、（　　　）に by または until を入れましょう。by が「〜までには」と最終期限を表すのに対し、until は「〜までずっと」と動作や状態の継続を表します。その違いを確認しましょう。

(1) お名前が呼ばれるまでこちらでお待ちください。
　　Please wait here (　　　　) I call your name.

(2) 「検査結果はいつ分かりますか？」「検査結果は正午までに出るでしょう。」
　　"When will the results be ready?" "They will be ready (　　　　) noon."

 **Dialogue**

A = Patient　B = Receptionist　C = Nurse　D = Doctor

　　　　　　　　　　　　　　　　　　　　　　　　　　　　　　Audio 1-43

At the reception desk

A: Good morning. I am here for a gastroscopy. I have an appointment at 9:00 a.m. My name is Richard Cook.

B: Ah, yes. Here you are, Mr. Cook. Please come in and wait. The nurse will be with you shortly.

A: Thank you.

In the treatment room

C: Good morning, Mr. Cook. How are you feeling today?

A: I'm feeling pretty nervous. ①<u>This is my first time to have a gastroscopy exam.</u>

C: Don't worry, your doctor is extremely skilled. Do your best to relax and not worry. Things will be fine. Just let me explain the procedure.

A: Okay.

After the nurse's explanation

C: Okay, Mr. Cook. ②<u>Now, it's time for your shot.</u> This shot is what's called an intramuscular injection. The shot may hurt, so please relax and be patient.

A: Ouch.

C: All finished. Please hold this cotton ball against your arm.

A: Okay.

C: Next, you'll need to take two spoonfuls of this liquid medicine. It will numb your throat. It's a little hard to swallow, so please be careful and go slowly.

In the examination room

C: Mr. Cook, we are ready now, so please come in. Please lie down on this bed on your right side so that you can watch these monitors.

A: Like this?

C: Yes, that's perfect. Your doctor will be here soon. Please relax. I'll be here while you're going through the examination. So let me know if you have any questions or concerns.

A: Okay, thank you.

After the gastroscopy

D: Well, all the tests are finished. Please come back tomorrow so that we can look at the results together. Please relax here for half an hour, and then if you feel fine, you are free to go home.

A: Okay doctor. Thank you. I'll see you tomorrow.

D: Take care of yourself, Mr. Cook.

※ intramuscular injection「筋肉注射」

Vocabulary Check　　　Audio 1-44

(1)～(6) に合う語義をそれぞれ (a)～(f) から選びなさい。

(1) go through　(　)　　(2) numb　(　)
(3) patient　(　)　　(4) shot　(　)
(5) skilled　(　)　　(6) swallow　(　)

(a) 注射　(b) 腕がいい　(c) 我慢強い　(d) (治療などを) 受ける　(e) 麻痺させる　(f) 飲み込む

time を使った「〜回目」、「初めて」を表す表現　　Audio 1-45

Dialogue 中の下線部①を参照し、音声を聴いて、(　)を埋めましょう。

(1) 富士山に登るのは今回が2回目です。
　　This is (　) (　) time (　) (　) Mt. Fuji.

(2) ニューヨークへいらしたのは今回が初めてですか。
　　Is this (　) (　) (　) to New York?

(3) ボランティアとして働くのは今回が初めてです。
　　This is (　) (　) time I've worked as a volunteer.

(4) 祖父に会ったのはあの時が最後だった。
　　(　) (　) (　) (　) time I met my grandfather.

 「〜する時だ」を表す表現　　Audio 1-46

Dialogue 中の下線部②を参照し、音声を聴いて、リピートしましょう。

(1) Now it's time for a lunch break. (さあ、昼休みだよ。)

(2) Now it's time for the evening news. (夕方のニュースの時間です。)

(3) It's about time for us to leave. (そろそろ帰る時間です。)

(4) It's high time you got to work.
　　(もうとっくに仕事にとりかかっていないといけない時ですよ。)

Everyday Conversation

At the Airport Lobby　　Audio 1-47

A = Clerk　B = Passenger

At a check-in counter

A: Welcome to Bluebird Airlines! ①<u>Let me help you with your check-in today.</u>

B: Thank you very much.

A: Can I see your ticket and passport, please?

B: Yes, of course. ②<u>Here you are.</u>

A: Thank you. You're flying direct to Boston, correct?

B: Yes, that's correct.

A: ③<u>Well, your plane is scheduled to depart on time.</u> Would you like a window seat or an aisle seat?

B: An aisle seat, please.

A: How much baggage will you be checking in?

B: Just one piece. And of course I also have this carry-on bag.

A: Alright. Then, could you please place it on the scale?

B: Okay. ④<u>Here you go.</u>

A: Thank you. Great, your bag is 13.5kg, so you will not have to pay any extra for excess luggage.

B: Good.

A: Right, your bag is checked in and here is your boarding pass. Please be at gate 37 at least fifteen minutes prior to departure.

B: Thank you very much.

A: You're welcome. Have a wonderful flight to America!

※ check in「搭乗手続きをする」 on time = on schedule「定刻に」 fly direct to ~「~へ直行便で行く」
depart (⇔ arrive)「出発する」 an aisle seat「通路側の席」 check in baggage「荷物を預ける」
carry-on luggage「機内持ち込み手荷物」 place「置く」 at least「少なくとも」 prior to ~ = before「~より前に」

 help … with ~ / help … do　　　　　　　　　🔊 Audio 1-48

Dialogue 中の下線部①を参照し、音声を聴いて、リピートしましょう。

(1) I'll help you with these bags.

(2) I'll help you carry these bags.

 相手に物を差し出す表現　　　　　　　　　🔊 Audio 1-49

Dialogue 中の下線部②④を参照し、音声を聴いて、リピートしましょう。他にも Here it is. や Here they are. も使われます。

(1) "May I see the wine list?" "Sure. Here it is."
（「ワインリストをお願いします。」「かしこまりました。はい、どうぞ。」）

(2) "Can you pass me the pepper?" "Here you are."
（「胡椒をとってくれますか。」「はいどうぞ。」）

(3) "Two round-trip tickets, please?" "Okay. That's $18. Here they are."
（「往復切符を2枚下さい。」「分かりました。18ドルです。はい、どうぞ。」）

be scheduled to do を使った表現　　Audio 1-50

Dialogue 中の下線部③を参照し、音声を聴いて、(　)を埋めましょう。

(1) 社長と奥様は明日の午前にパリへ飛行機で行く予定です。
Our president and his wife (　) scheduled (　) (　) (　) Paris tomorrow morning.

(2) 国際学会が7月30日に予定されています。
The international conference (　) scheduled (　) July 30th.

Unit 6

医療活動には世界の共通語としての英語が必須

　派遣が決まったアフリカのコンゴ民主共和国は、フランス語が公用語でした。フランス語の発音には苦労しましたが、英語を勉強していたことがフランス語の勉強に役立ちました。特に医学用語は、語源がラテン語であり、英語もフランス語も似ているので覚えやすかったです。看護師や助産師は国際的な組織があり、国際学会が世界各国を巡回して開催されます。学会では世界の看護師たちが研究の成果を競い合います。学会はグローバル化にともなって現在は英語が公用語です。また、日本には数百万人の外国人が生活をしていますから、外来患者や入院患者の中にも外国人が増え、そのケアに関わる機会も増えています。世界の共通語としての英語はますます重要になっています。

空港や機内での重要表現　　　Audio 1-51

音声を聴いて、(　)に正しい語を埋めましょう。

(1)「預けるお荷物はございますか。」「はい、この二つです。」
　　"Do you have any baggage to (　　　) in?"
　　"Yes, these two (　　　), please."

(2) お客様の乗継便は機械のトラブルのため遅れています。
　　The departure of your connecting flight (　　) (　　　) due to mechanical problems.

(3) このことでご不便をおかけしまして、大変申し訳ございません。
　　We (　　　) (　　　) any inconvenience this may cause.

(4) ブルーバード・エアライン、ボストン行き327便をご利用いただきまして、誠にありがとうございます。
　　Welcome (　　　) Bluebird Airlines Flight 327 (　　　) (　　) Boston.

(5) ボストンまでの飛行時間は13時間を予定しております。
　　Our flight time to Boston (　　) (　　　) (　　) be thirteen hours.

(6) 手荷物は前の座席の下にお入れください。
　　Please (　　) your bags (　　　) the seats in front of you.

(7) 機内での喫煙はかたく禁じられております。
　　Smoking (　　) strictly (　　　) in this aircraft.

(8) 携帯電話やパソコンを含む全ての電子機器は必ず電源をお切りください。
　　All electronic devices, including cell phones and computers must (　　)
　　(　　　) (　　).

(9) 飛行機が揺れることが予想されます。
　　We (　　) (　　　) (　　) have some turbulence.

(10) お客様の安全のため、シートベルトを締めたままでお願いします。
　　For your safety, please (　　　) your seatbelts (　　　).

(11) 必ず税関申告書に記入してください。
　　Please make sure you (　　　) (　　　) this customs form.

(12)「今回の訪問の目的は何ですか？」「観光です。」
　　"What's the (　　　) of your visit?" "(　　　　)."

(13)「どれくらいの期間こちらに滞在予定ですか。」「10日間です。」
　　"(　　　) (　　　) are you going to stay here?" "(　　) days."

(14)〈税関で〉「何か申告するものはございますか。」「いいえ、ありません。」
　　"Do you have (　　　) (　　) (　　　)?" "No, I don't."

Unit 7 検査結果・入院

A = Doctor　B = Patient

🔊 Audio 1-52

In the doctor's office

A: Good morning, Mr. Cook. How are you feeling today?
B: Good morning, Dr. Clifford ... not so good.
A: I see. Okay let's go over the results of your tests. Yesterday we found some polyps and an ulcer in your stomach. From the biopsy, we confirmed that the tumors are benign, not malignant.
B: Oh, really? I'm so relieved!
A: Good, so you don't have to worry about an operation or anything like that.
B: Actually I was really shocked to hear that some polyps had been found. I became terribly upset when I thought about the possibility of cancer, so I couldn't sleep well last night.
A: ①<u>Mr. Cook, I have diagnosed your condition as a stomach ulcer.</u> So I think you should receive treatment in the hospital for a while. You will need to apply for admission to the hospital.
B: I see.
A: Great. Your nurse will explain about the hospitalization formalities.
B: Just as soon as I get back home, I'll get everything ready. Also I'll have to tell my family and my boss about it. How long will I need to be in hospital?
A: You'll need to stay one week.

Vocabulary Check　　　　　　　　　　　　　　　　　🔊 Audio 1-53

(1)～(14) に合う語義をそれぞれ (a)～(n) から選びなさい。

(1) admission　　　（ ）　　(2) apply for ~　　（ ）
(3) cancer　　　　（ ）　　(4) diagnose　　　（ ）
(5) formalities　　（ ）　　(6) malignant　　　（ ）
(7) operation　　　（ ）　　(8) possibility　　 （ ）
(9) preparation　　（ ）　　(10) tissue cell　　 （ ）
(11) treatment　　 （ ）　　(12) tumor　　　　 （ ）
(13) ulcer　　　　 （ ）　　(14) upset　　　　 （ ）

(a) 潰瘍	(b) 可能性	(c) 癌	(d) 手術	(e) 準備	(f) 正規の手続き
(g) 組織細胞	(h) 治療	(i) 腫瘍	(j) 入院	(k) 悪性の	(l) 動転した
(m) ～を申請する	(n) 診断する				

診断結果の表現　　　　　　　　　　　　　　　　　　🔊 Audio 1-54

Dialogue 中の下線部①を参照し、音声を聴いて、リピートしましょう。

(1) The doctor diagnosed the illness as a duodenal ulcer.
（医師はその病気を十二指腸潰瘍と診断した。）

(2) She was diagnosed with diabetes.（彼女は糖尿病と診断された。）

Everyday Conversation

At a Fast-food Restaurant　　　　　　　　　　　　🔊 Audio 1-55

A = Steve　B = Lisa

Lisa is going to the clinic's Sunshine Café.

A: Hey, Lisa. Are you going to Sunshine Café now?
B: Hi, Steve. Yes, I am.
A: Me, too! ①Would you mind if I joined you?
B: Sure, that would be great. Steve, we had a wonderful time last Sunday. I was happy to see Ken and Jane, too. Thank you so much.
A: Yeah, we had a lot of fun. Your apple pie was delicious. ②I was happy to see that you're good at baking.
B: Thank you. Let's get together soon!

※ have a good time「楽しい時間を過ごす」　have a lot of fun「楽しむ」　get together「集まる」

許可を求める表現

Dialogue 中の下線部①の表現を使い、(　　) 内を埋めましょう。

★ join よりも joined と過去形にする方がさらに丁寧になります。

(1)「窓を開けてもよろしいですか。」「はい、いいですよ。」
　"Would you mind (　　) (　　) (　　) the window?"
　"(　　), I wouldn't."

(2)「ここに座ってもよろしいですか。」「いいですよ。」
　"Would you mind (　　) (　　) (　　) here?" "I don't mind."

「〜が得意だ」という表現　　　Audio 1-56

Dialogue 中の下線部②の表現を参照し、音声を聴いて、リピートしましょう。

★ S is good at 〜 と S is good with 〜 は「S は〜が上手だ、得意だ」という意味ですが、at は「技術」について、with は「扱い」について得意であることを表します。

(1) You're good at speaking English.（あなたは英語を話すのが得意なんですね。）

(2) You're good at cooking.（あなたは料理が得意なんですね。）

(3) I'm not good with machines.（私は機械を扱うのが苦手なんです。）

Ordering (at Sunshine Café)　　　Audio 1-57

A = Staff　B = Steve　C = Lisa

A: Hello. What can I do for you today?
B: ③Hi, I'd like a large-size coffee. How about you, Lisa?
C: ④Oh, I'll have a café latte, please.
A: What (①　　　　) would you like, ma'am?
C: Medium, please.
A: All right. How about a muffin or a donut?
C: Wow, they look delicious. I'll have a blueberry muffin.
A: Good choice! How about you, sir?
B: Hmmm, I'd like a cinnamon roll.
A: Good. Anything else?
B: That's (②　　　　).
A: ⑤For here or to go?
B: We're going to (③　　　　) (④　　　　), please.
A: Okay, that'll be $9.25.

B: ⑥It's my treat, Lisa. I've got it.
C: Oh, thank you. That's very kind of you, Steve. ⑦Next time it's on me.
A: Sir, here's your (⑤   ): 75 cents. Please pick up your orders at that counter over there.
B: Thanks.

Listening Exercise

❶ダイアログの音声を聴いて、(①   ) ~ (⑤   ) に入る語を書きましょう。

❷ (1) ~ (4) の文を読み、本文の内容に合うものにはT（True）、当てはまらない場合はF（False）を［ ］に書きなさい。

(1) [   ] Lisa orders a large-size café latte.
(2) [   ] Steve likes cinnamon rolls but doesn't like muffins.
(3) [   ] They are going to eat in the café.
(4) [   ] They pay separately.

 ファーストフード店やレストランでの表現　　　Audio 1-58

音声を聴いて、リピートしましょう。

❶ Dialogue 中の下線部③④の表現を参照しましょう。

(1) "I'll have a hamburger, French fries and Coke." "Sure. That's $7.59."
（「ハンバーガーとフライドポテトとコーラをお願いします。」
「かしこまりました。7ドル59セントです。」）

❷ Dialogue 中の下線部⑤の表現を参照しましょう。

(1) "For here or to go?" "To go, please."
（「店内でお召し上がりですか、それともテイクアウトにしますか。」「テイクアウトにします。」）

❸ Dialogue 中の下線部⑥⑦の表現を参照しましょう。

(1) This is on me. （これは私がおごりますね。）

(2) I'll treat you tonight. （今夜は私がごちそうするわ。）

(3) Thank you so much. I'll pay next time. （本当にありがとう。次回は私が払うわね。）

(4) Let's split the bill. （割り勘にしましょう。）

Unit 8 術前・術後

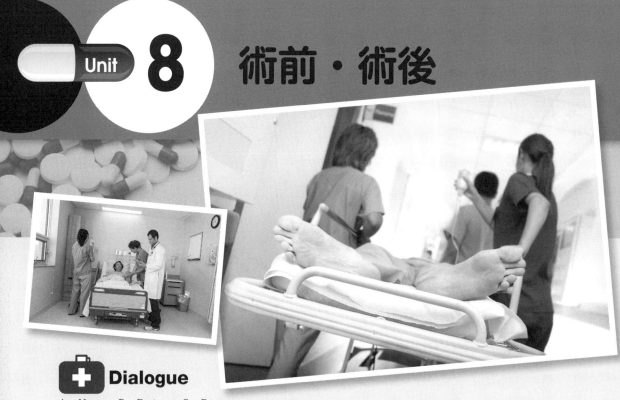

Dialogue

A = Nurse   B = Patient   C = Doctor

🔊 Audio 2-01

Pre-operation

A: ① Ms. Smith, I will be bringing you to the operating room on the stretcher.
B: Thank you. How long will the surgery take?
A: About two hours.
B: Oh, I see.
A: Okay, we are all ready. Let's go then.

Post-operation consultation

A: ② Jane, the surgery went well.
B: Oh, thank you. ③ I'm relieved to hear that.
A: ④ The doctor will be coming here soon to talk to you about it.
B: Thank you.

A few minutes later

C: How are you feeling now?
B: I'm OK, but I feel numbness in my legs.
C: I see.
B: I'm feeling really depressed.
C: I understand your feelings. I'm afraid you'll be annoyed to find you can't move at all. But all the staff will assist you from now on. Anyway, I think you need to sleep well tonight.
B: Okay.

C: If you need anything else, please call the nurses anytime.
B: Yes, I will.
C: Well then have a good night.
B: Thank you, Dr. Jones.

The next morning

C: Good morning, Jane. Did you sleep well last night?
B: Good morning, Dr. Jones. I don't think so. I'm still sleepy now.
C: I see. How are you feeling?
B: I feel bad, and sometimes I have acute pain.
C: I see. You are on an IV drip which relieves your pain. Please let us know if you feel something is wrong.
B: Okay, I will. ⑤<u>I feel like crying because I can't do anything by myself.</u>
C: Jane, it will take time for the wound to heal completely, but please don't worry. That's a normal part of the healing process.
B: I know.
C: ⑥<u>You seem to think it's boring to lie in bed all day long.</u> But you can read, watch TV and do anything you want. It is important for you to relieve your stress during your time in the hospital. Take it easy, Jane.
B: I'll give it a try. Thank you for your advice, Dr. Jones.

Vocabulary Check Audio 2-02

(1)〜(10) に合う語義をそれぞれ (a)〜(j) から選びなさい。

(1) acute   ( )   (2) annoy   ( )
(3) anyway   ( )   (4) assist   ( )
(5) boring   ( )   (6) depress   ( )
(7) negatively( )   (8) numbness ( )
(9) relieve   ( )   (10) surgery ( )

(a) 外科手術　(b) 無感覚　(c) 退屈させる　(d) 激しい　(e) いずれにしても
(f) 悲観的に　(g) 安心させる、取り除く　(h) いらいらさせる　(i) 助ける
(j) 憂鬱にさせる

Useful Expressions

❶ Dialogue 中の下線部①④の未来進行形を参照し、音声を聴いて、(　　) を埋めましょう。

(1) 10 時半までに 7 番ゲートにお越しください。飛行機は定刻に出発予定です。
Please be at Gate 7 by 10:30. The flight (　　) (　　) (　　) on time.

(2) 私たちの便は予定通り 9 時半に出発する予定です。
Our flight (　　) (　　) (　　) on schedule at 9:30.

(3) 当機は間もなく離陸します。
We (　　) (　　) (　　) (　　) shortly.

❷ Dialogue 中の下線部②の「物事が進行している表現」を参照し、音声を聴いて、リピートしましょう。

(1) "How's everything going?" "Everything is going well so far."
（「全て順調ですか？」「今のところうまくいっています。」）

(2) "How did the presentation go?" "It went pretty well."
（「プレゼンはどうだった？」「かなりうまくいったよ。」）

❸ Dialogue 中の下線部③を参照し、音声を聴いて、(　　) を埋めましょう。

(1) その知らせを聞いてほっとしました。
I (　　) relieved to (　　) that news.

(2) あなたが快方に向かっていると知って、本当にうれしいです。
I'm really (　　) (　　) (　　) that you are getting better.

(3) このような機会をいただけてうれしいです。
I'm (　　) (　　) (　　) such an opportunity.

(4) 彼が事故に遭ったと知って、とても悲しいです。
I'm so (　　) (　　) (　　) that he had an accident.

❹ Dialogue 中の下線部⑤の「～したい気がする」という表現を参照し、音声を聴いて、(　　) を埋めましょう。

(1) 今食べる気がしないんだ。I don't feel like (　　) now.

(2) 出かける気分ではないよ。I don't feel like (　　) (　　).

(3) 今、散歩に出かけたい気分だ。I feel like (　　) (　　) (　　) now.

❺ Dialogue 中の下線部⑥を参照し、音声を聴いて、(　　　)を埋めましょう。

(1) 痩せてきているようですね。
　　You seem (　　) (　　) (　　　) (　　　).

(2) 彼は病気のようです。
　　He (　　　) (　　　) (　　) (　　　).

(3) 彼女は現代美術が好きではないようです。
　　She (　　　) (　　　) (　　) like modern art.

(4) きちんと治っているようです。
　　It seems (　　) (　　) (　　　) nicely.

術前・術後のやりとりの表現　　　Audio 2-04

音声を聴いて、(　　　)に入る語を書き入れましょう。

(1) 車いすに座るのをお手伝いします。
　　Let me (　　) (　　) (　　) in this wheel chair.

(2) トイレには行きましたか？
　　Did you go to the (　　　)?

(3) 毎日朝、ガーゼを交換します。
　　I will (　　　) your dressing daily in the mornings.

(4) 何か必要なものがあれば、お知らせください。
　　Well, please (　　) (　　) (　　) if there is anything else you need.

(5) 今のところ、大丈夫です。今は痛みはありません。
　　It (　　) (　　) (　　) (　　). There is no pain right now.

(6) 傷口がどのように治っているか確認しますね。
　　May I look to see (　　) (　　) (　　)?

(7) 傷口は良くなっているようです。
　　Your (　　　) (　　　) better.

(8) ガーゼを外しますから、じっとしていてください。
　　Let me (　　　) the dressing. Please stay (　　　).

(9) 明日の午前中に経過について説明します。
　　I will explain the (　　　) to you tomorrow morning.

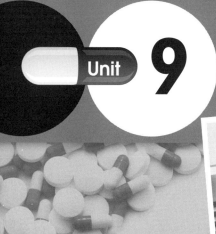

Unit 9 待合室での会話

A = Lisa (outpatient)　　B = Ken (visitor)

🔊 Audio 2-05

Ken is going to a general hospital to visit Jane.

A: Ken! What are you doing here?

B: Oh, Lisa! I'm here to see Jane.

A: Oh, really? Is she here? What happened to her?

B: Actually, she had a car accident yesterday and broke both her legs, so she was brought here to have an emergency operation.

A: Oh, that's terrible. I didn't know that. Is she going to be okay?

B: Well, I heard she was feeling depressed because she wouldn't be able to move around for a while. The doctor told her it would probably take a couple of months for her to recover fully.

A: Oh, I'm sorry to hear that. I'll also go and see her later.

B: Good. I hope we can help cheer her up. By the way, why are you here?

A: ① <u>Actually, I'm here to get my flu vaccination, because students are advised to do so at my nursing school.</u> It's good to be safe, right?

B: I see. Okay, it's 3:00 p.m. now. Visiting hours have started!

Vocabulary Check　　　Audio 2-06

(1)〜(6) に合う語義をそれぞれ (a)〜(f) から選びなさい。

(1) break　　　(　)　　　(2) cheer　　　(　)
(3) emergency　(　)　　　(4) flu　　　　(　)
(5) recover　　(　)　　　(6) vaccination (　)

(a) インフルエンザ　(b) 予防接種　(c) 緊急の　(d) 折る、骨折する
(e) 快復する　　　　(f) 元気づける

be advised to do を使った表現　　　Audio 2-07

Dialogue 中の下線部①を参照し、音声を聴いて、リピートしましょう。

(1) Passengers are advised to always keep their personal belongings with them.
（乗客の皆様は常に自分の持ち物は持ち歩くようにお願いします。）

(2) We were advised to make reservations in advance.
（我々は事前に予約するように勧められた。）

病気の説明

以下は病気の説明です。病名を語群から選び、(　) に書きましょう。

(1) (　　　　　) an infectious viral disease causing fever and a red rash, typically occurring in childhood.

(2) (　　　　　) a serious medical condition in which the appendix becomes inflamed and painful.

(3) (　　　　　) a respiratory condition marked by attacks of spasm in the bronchi of the lungs, causing difficulty in breathing.

● appendicitis　　● asthma　　● measles

体調やけがの状態を説明する表現

❶ (　) に入る語を下の語郡から選びなさい。

(1) I have a headache and feel a little (　　　　). (頭痛がするし、熱っぽいな。)

(2) I feel (　　　　) and have a (　　　　) nose. (寒気がして、鼻水が出ます。)

(3) I have hay fever, so my eyes are (　　　　) and I often (　　　　).
(私は花粉症なので、目がかゆいし、よくくしゃみが出ます。)

(4) I have (　　　　), so it's terrible. (下痢の症状があり、とても辛いです。)

(5) I feel really tired and (　　　　). (本当に疲れていて力が入りません。)

(6) She is three months (　　　　). (彼女は妊娠3ヶ月です。)

(7) He turned out to be (　　　　) with flu.
(彼はインフルエンザに感染していることが判明した。)

> ●chilly　●diarrhea　●feverish　●infected　●itchy
> ●pregnant　●runny　●sneeze　●weak

❷ (　) に入る語を下の語郡から選びなさい。

(1) I cut my finger with a knife and it's (　　　　).
(包丁で指を切り、出血しています。)

(2) I (　　　　) myself when I touched the hot pan.
(熱い鍋に触れて、やけどしました。)

(3) I (　　　　) my ankle and it's swollen. (足首を捻挫して、腫れています。)

(4) I (　　　　) my neck. (首を寝違えてしまいました。)

(5) My left calf is (　　　　) up. (左のふくらはぎがつっています。)

(6) I was (　　　　) by a bee. (蜂に刺されました。)

(7) I (　　　　) my arm. (腕を骨折した。)

> ●bleeding　●broke　●burned　●cramping　●sprained　●stung　●twisted

Everyday Conversation

Buying Tickets

🔊 Audio 2-08

A = Clerk   B = Audience

At the box office

A: Next, please. Good evening, sir. How may I help you?
B: Can I have a ticket for the 7:00 p.m. showing of this movie?
A: I'm afraid the tickets for 7:00 p.m. (①   ) (②   ) (③   ) and it has already started.
B: Oh, I see.
A: We have a 9:00 p.m. showing, and the tickets are still (④   ).
B: That's good. I'd like to see that one then.
A: Sure. That'll be $9.25.

A = Clerk   B = Passenger

At the ticket counter in the station

A: Good morning. How can I help you?
B: Good morning. Actually, I don't know (⑤   ) (⑥   ) (⑦   ) a ticket from the ticket-vending machine, so can I get one here?
A: Of course.
B: I'd like to get a ticket to Hartford.
A: Okay. One way or round trip?
B: One way, please.
A: Let's see. The (⑧   ) train has just left here, so the next one is at (⑨   ). Is that okay with you?
B: Yes, I'll take that one, please.
A: Sure. That'll be $15. Cash or credit card?
B: Cash, please.
A: Here's your change and this is your ticket.
B: Thank you.

❶音声を聴いて、①〜⑨の(　)に入る語を書きましょう。
❷ペアになって、会話を発音練習してみましょう。

Unit 10 清拭

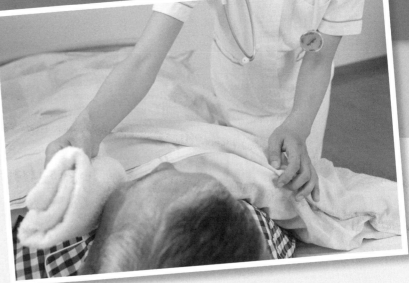

Dialogue

A = Nurse   B = Patient

🔊 Audio 2-09

A: Hi, Jane. How are you feeling today?
B: I'm okay, thanks.
A: Good. Now it's time for your bed bath. Can you clean yourself with these hot towels?
B: Yes, I can.
A: ①<u>When you finish cleaning yourself, then I'll wipe your back, legs and so on.</u>
B: Thank you.

Ten minutes later

A: Jane, are you done?
B: Yes, I've almost finished.
A: Okay. Let me wipe the rest of your body. I will also help you change your gown.
B: Thank you. ②<u>I wish I could take a shower.</u>
A: I'm sorry, but you can't. ③<u>Actually, this morning Dr. Jones told me to wash your hair.</u>
B: Oh, really? I'm so glad to hear that. I haven't washed my hair for five days.
A: Later I will take you to the bathroom in a wheelchair. In the meantime, our staff will change your sheets and pillow case as usual.
B: Thank you very much.

重要表現

Audio 2-10

❶ Dialogue 中の下線部①の動名詞の表現を参照し、音声を聴いて、(　　) を埋めましょう。

(1) この本を読み終えましたか。
　　Have you (　　　) (　　　) this book?

(2) 咳が止まりません。
　　I can't (　　　) (　　　).

(3) 食べ過ぎは控えた方がいいですよ。
　　You should (　　　) (　　　) too much.

(4) 父は禁煙した。
　　My father (　　　) (　　　) (　　　).

(5) 突然、雨が降り出した。
　　It (　　　) (　　　) suddenly.

(6) 以前どこかで彼女に会ったことを覚えています。
　　I (　　　) (　　　) (　　　) somewhere before.

(7) その患者は毎日歩く練習をしています。
　　The patient (　　　) (　　　) every day.

❷ Dialogue 中の下線部②の仮定法過去の表現を参照し、音声を聴いて、リピートしましょう。

★ I wish + S + 過去形で、「～であればいいのになあ」と、現在において実現できそうにない願望を表します。

(1) I wish I were energetic like you. (あなたのように私もエネルギッシュだといいのになあ。)

(2) I wish I could go to the concert with you. (私もあなたたちと一緒にコンサートに行けたらいいのになあ。)

(3) I wish you were a doctor. (あなたが医者であればいいのになあ。)

❸ Dialogue 中の下線部③の表現を参照し、音声を聴いて、(　　) を埋めましょう。

(1) 薬剤師は私に正しく薬を服用するように言いました。
　　The pharmacist (　　　) (　　　) (　　　) (　　　) medicine properly.

(2) 私は看護師にもう一枚毛布を持ってくるように頼みました。
　　I (　　　) the (　　　) (　　　) (　　　) another blanket.

(3) 受付係が私に保険証を持ってくるように言った。
　　The receptionist (　　　) (　　　) (　　　) (　　　) my insurance card with me.

(4) 私は弟に雨が降るといけないから傘を持っていくように言いました。
　　I (　　　) my brother (　　　) (　　　) an umbrella (　　　) (　　　) just in case.

Everyday Conversation

Checking In

🔊 Audio 2-11

A = Receptionist   B = Guest

At the front desk

A: Good afternoon, ma'am. How may I help you?
B: I'd like to check in, please.
A: Certainly. Do you (①) a reservation?
B: Yes, I do. My name is Lisa Clifford.
A: Let me see. Ah, yes. Ms. Clifford, you'll be staying with us for (②) nights.
B: That's right.
A: Thank you. A (③) room for $180 per night. How would you like to pay for this, ma'am?
B: By credit card.
A: That's fine. May I see your credit card and passport, please?
B: Okay. Here you are.
A: Thank you, ma'am. Let me check them, and could you fill out this registration form, please?
B: Sure.
A: Alright, here you are; your credit card and passport.
B: Thank you. I've finished (④) (⑤) (⑥).
A: Well, may I have your (⑦) here, please?
B: Sure.
A: Perfect. Your room number is (⑧). Here is your room (⑨). Breakfast is served from 6:30 a.m. to 10:30 a.m. at the restaurant on the (⑩) floor. Do you have any questions?
B: Yes, I'd like to know the check-out time?
A: The check-out time is 11:00 a.m.
B: I see.
A: The porter will take your baggage to your room. Have a nice stay.
B: Thank you.

❶音声を聴いて、①〜⑩の(　　)に入る語を書きましょう。

❷ペアになって、会話を発音練習してみましょう。

❸ホテルのフロントとのやりとりの表現について、(　　　)に正しい語を埋めましょう。

(1)「今夜、空いている部屋はありますか？」「申し訳ございませんが、当ホテルは今夜は満室です。」
　　"Do you have any (　　　　　) for tonight?"
　　"I'm sorry, we are (　　　　　) tonight."

(2)「すみませんが、シャワーから水が出ません。」
　　「申し訳ございません。しばらくお待ちいただけますか。すぐに係の者がそちらに伺います。」
　　"Excuse me, but (　　　) (　　) no water in the shower."
　　"I'm sorry, could you wait for a while? I'll (　　　　) someone up to your room."

Unit 10

清拭

HIVに対する正しい知識の普及が重要

　1981年にエイズが確認されてから35年になりますが、まだHIV（エイズウイルス）の特効薬は見つかっていません。先進国では抗エイズ剤により延命が可能になりましたが、途上国ではいまだに「死の病」です。先進国は「世界基金」を設立し途上国への支援を行なっていますが、道路や電気などのインフラの不備や医療者の不足のため、農村部までは薬が行き届いていません。また、HIVは感染経路が明確で、予防可能な感染症であるという、正しい知識の普及が重要です。識字率が低い学校や地域に出かけ、テレビ、ラジオ、ビデオ、紙芝居、演劇など様々な媒体を使って啓発教育を行なっていますが、途上国でいまだに感染拡大が続いている原因は、HIVに対して無知であることと、予防ができていないことです。

Unit 11 リハビリ

Dialogue

A = Physical Therapist   B = Patient

Audio 2-12

A: Hi, Ms. Smith. I'm happy to say, you're gradually recovering from your injuries. Dr. Jones told me that we should start focusing on your rehabilitation.

B: Yes, he spoke to me after looking at my X-rays yesterday. This morning he finally took my casts off. What a relief! I'm happier now, but it's been a tough time.

A: I can understand how you're feeling. Has the pain become more tolerable?

B: Yes, it has. Much more manageable. But because I've been in a wheelchair the past month, I'm worried about my rehab. I'm wondering how long it'll be before I'll walk normally again?

A: Well, from previous rehab cases for this kind of injury, you can expect to be walking again normally in a month. We'll work together on this, okay?

B: Thank you. I'll work hard and keep at it until I am back on my feet!

A: Great. Okay then, let's get started!

The next day

A: ①Okay Jane, today you will stand up while holding onto the parallel bars and then slowly learn to walk on crutches.

B: Right.

A: First of all, I'd like to look at your feet and legs? Can you please get out of the wheelchair and move to that chair? Oh, and take off your slippers too, please.

B: Made it!

A: Good. Now, place your feet up on this stool.

B: Okay.

A: Yeah, perfect. ②I see they are still a little swollen, aren't they? Do you feel any pain?

B: Yes, a little. Especially around my ankles.

A: Well, I'm going to massage your feet and legs for about ten minutes. Please tell me if you have any pain while I'm doing it.

B: Okay.

A: The massage will help your circulation and loosen up the leg muscles. So just relax, please.

B: Oh, that feels great. It's very relaxing. Thank you.

Ten minutes later

A: Good! Next, can you please move your feet to the left and then the right?

B: Like this?

A: Yes, exactly. Now move your feet up and down.

B: Is this okay?

A: Yes. Now, can you try to stand up while using my hands and arms for support?

B: Whoops!

A: It's okay, you're safe. Now let's try stepping forward slowly.

B: Oh no, I can't move. This is scary. I feel like I've forgotten how to walk!

A: Everyone feels the same at first. ③From now on, every day you will spend about an hour with our staff practicing how to walk.

※ first of all 「まず始めに」 at first 「最初は」

Vocabulary Check 🔊 Audio 2-13

(1) ～ (10) の語義に合うものをそれぞれ (a) ～ (j) から選びなさい。

(1) ankle   (　)　　(2) cast   (　)
(3) circulation (　)　　(4) injury   (　)
(5) loosen up   (　)　　(6) manageable (　)
(7) muscle   (　)　　(8) scary   (　)
(9) tough   (　)　　(10) warmth   (　)

> (a) 足首　　(b) 温かさ　　(c) ギプス　　(d) 筋肉　　(e) 怪我　　(f) 血行
> (g) 怖い　　(h) ほどほどの、手に負える　　(i) つらい　　(j) ほぐす、ゆるめる

Unit 11

重要表現 🔊 Audio 2-14

❶ Dialogue 中の下線部①の「練習して〜ができるようになる」という表現を参照し、音声を聴いて、(　) を埋めましょう。

(1) 私は英語で自分のことをもっと自由に表現できるようになるために、一生懸命英語を勉強しています。
　　I've been studying English hard to (　　　)(　　)(　　　) myself (　　) English more freely.

(2) 息子はようやく泳げるようになりました。
　　My son (　　)(　　)(　　　) finally.

❷ Dialogue 中の下線部②の表現を参照し、音声を聴いて、リピートしましょう。

(1) Your eyes are swollen. Are you alright?（目が腫れていますよ。大丈夫ですか？）

(2) Your tonsils seem to be swollen.（扁桃腺が腫れているようですね。）

❸ Dialogue 中の下線部③の表現を参照し、音声を聴いて、(　　　) を埋めましょう。

(1) 今週末は図書館で研究に時間を費やすつもりです。
　　I'm going to (　　　) this (　　　)(　　　) research in the library.

(2) 妹は空いている時間をよくボランティア活動に参加することに費やします。
　　My sister often (　　　) her free time (　　　)(　　) volunteer activities.

(3) 今日の午後はビーチでのんびりして過ごしたよ。
　　I (　　　) this afternoon (　　　) on the beach.

Everyday Conversation

At a Foreign Exchange Office

🔊 Audio 2-15

A = Clerk   B = Customer

A: Good afternoon. May I help you?
B: Yes, I'd like to exchange some yen into dollars. What's the exchange rate today?
A: One dollar is 106.53 yen, including our commission fee. How much yen would you like to exchange, ma'am?
B: Thirty thousand yen, please.
A: ① <u>Okay. Let's see…that'll be $281.61. Here you go: four fifty-dollar bills, two twenty-dollar bills, four ten-dollar bills, one one-dollar bill, six dimes and one penny, okay? Here is your receipt. Thank you.</u>
B: Great. Thanks.

※ exchange「両替をする」 exchange rate「為替レート」 commission fee「手数料」 bill「紙幣」

❶アメリカの硬貨について、(a)〜(e)の中から正しいものを選びなさい。

(1) quarter   (　)   (2) penny   (　)
(3) nickel   (　)   (4) half dollar (　)
(5) dime   (　)

(a) 1セント硬貨 (b) 5セント硬貨 (c) 10セント硬貨 (d) 25セント硬貨 (e) 50セント硬貨

❷下線部①では、日本円をドルに両替をしてもらっているところです。日本語に訳しましょう。

_____

_____

_____

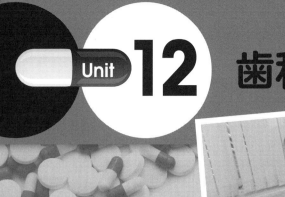

Unit 12 歯科治療

Dialogue

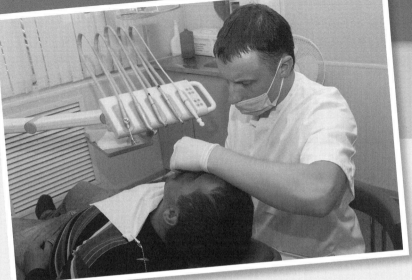

A = Patient B = Doctor C = Nurse D = Dentist

Audio 2-16

A: Dr. Jones, I'd like to see a dentist because one of my fillings came out this morning.

B: Oh, I see. I'll have the nurse make a dental appointment for you.

A: Thank you.

B: Can you walk to the dental department on crutches by yourself? Of course you can use a wheel chair, and your nurse will take you there if you ask.

A: No, I think I can go there by myself. I've been practicing walking on crutches for a week.

B: Good, but please be careful.

Thirty minutes later

C: Jane, I've made an appointment for you at 2:30.

A: Thank you very much.

C: Oh, and please remember to go for rehab after that.

A: Okay, I will.

At the dental department

D: I see your filling has come out. ①Okay, let's take a look…open wide please?

A: Okay.

D: Right I see it. Let me examine if you have any new cavities.

A: Yes, please.

D: I see there is also a small cavity on the right lower back tooth as well.

A: ②So that's why I sometimes feel pain when I drink anything cold.

D: Okay, rinse, please.

A: All right.

D: Ms. Smith, you have tartar on your teeth. However, first I'll make the fillings for your teeth and then the dental hygienist will clean and polish your teeth. ③I recommend that you have regular dental checkups to keep your teeth clean from now on.

A: Yes, I will do that.

Vocabulary Check　　Audio 2-17

(1)～(8) に合う語義をそれぞれ (a)～(h) から選び、記号で答えなさい。

(1) cavity　　(　)　　(2) checkup　　(　)
(3) crutches　　(　)　　(4) department　　(　)
(5) filling　　(　)　　(6) hygienist　　(　)
(7) rinse　　(　)　　(8) tartar　　(　)

(a) 衛生士　(b) 科　(c) 検診　(d) 歯石　(e) 詰め物　(f) 松葉杖
(g) 虫歯　(h) ゆすぐ、すすぐ

Useful Expressions　　Audio 2-18

❶ Dialogue 中の下線部①の表現を参照し、音声を聴いて、(　　) を埋めましょう。

(1) ちょっとこれを見てくれない？
　　Can you (　　) a (　　) look (　　) this?

(2) このサンプルをもっと詳しく見てみます。
　　I'll (　　) (　　) (　　) look at this sample.

❷ Dialogue 中の下線部②の表現を参照し、音声を聴いて、リピートしましょう。

(1) "I have a bad cold." "So that's why you didn't come to work."
（「ひどい風邪をひいてるんだ。」「それで仕事を休んだのね。」）

(2) "Dr. Clifford always listens to her patients."
"That's why they trust her so much."
（「クリフォード先生はいつも患者さんの話を親身になって聞いてあげているわ。」「だから患者さんたちは先生に信頼を寄せているのね。」）

(3) "I heard Ken lived in New York until he was 12 years old."
"That's why he speaks English fluently."
(「ケンは12歳までニューヨークで暮していたそうよ。」「そういうわけで彼は英語を流暢に話せるんだね。」)

❸ Dialogue 中の下線部③の表現を参照し、音声を聴いて、リピートしましょう。

★ that 節の中では動詞の原形を用います。

Unit 12

(1) My doctor recommended that I have a thorough physical checkup.
(医師は私に人間ドックを受けるように勧めました。)

(2) The doctor recommended that he refrain from drinking alcohol.
(医者は彼に飲酒を控えるよう勧めました。)

(3) Could you recommend a good dentist around here?"
(この辺りでいい歯医者さんを紹介していただけますか？)

(4) Can you recommend a good Italian restaurant near here?
(この近くで美味しいイタリア料理のレストランを教えてくれませんか？)

(5) What would you recommend for dinner? (ディナーは何がお勧めですか？)

歯科治療に関する表現 Audio 2-19

音声を聴いて、(　　)に入る語を書き入れましょう。

(1) このデンタルリンスで虫歯を防ぐことができます。
　　This dental rinse can (　　　　　) (　　　　　).

(2) 虫歯の治療をする必要があります。
　　I need to (　　　　　) (　　　　　) for a cavity.

(3) 3本虫歯があります。
　　I (　　　　　) three (　　　　　).

(4) 歯磨きする時に歯茎から出血します。
　　My gums (　　　　　) when I (　　　　　) my (　　　　　).

(5) 親知らずを抜いてもらいました。
　　I had my wisdom tooth (　　　　　) (　　　　　).

(6) 一日一回デンタルフロスを使った方がいいですよ。
　　You should use dental floss (　　　　　) (　　　　　) (　　　　　).

(7) 歯がひどく痛みます。
　　I (　　　　　) a bad (　　　　　).

(8) この海外旅行保険は歯の治療も適用されます。
　　This overseas travel insurance (　　　　　) dental (　　　　　).

Everyday Conversation

Taking a Taxi or Getting on the Bus

🔊 Audio 2-20

A = Passenger   B = Driver

A: Excuse me, but does this bus go to the National Museum?
B: No it doesn't. Take the 52A bus, please. The bus stop is over there. Can you see it?
A: Yes, I can. Thank you.

A = Passenger   B = Receptionist

At the airport

A: Excuse me, the guidebook says this hotel has a shuttle bus that does an airport pick-up.
B: Well, I'll take a look…yes, that's right.
A: How often does the shuttle bus run?
B: Let me check. It runs every 20 minutes.
A: I see. So where can we find the shuttle bus?
B: The bus stop is just outside that exit door. You can't miss it.
A: Thank you very much.

A = Passenger   B = Receptionist   C = Driver

At the front desk

A: Excuse me, could you please call a taxi for me?
B: Certainly. Please wait in the lobby until I call you.
A: Thanks.

A few minutes later

C: Good morning, ma'am. Where to?
A: The International Convention Center, please.
C: Sure.
A: Could you please tell me how much the fare from here is?
C: I think it's about $15. There is not much traffic on the roads now, so it will be an easy journey.
A: Great, thanks.

❶公共の交通機関を利用する際の表現です。ペアになって練習しましょう。

Unit 12

歯科治療

Unit 13 回復・退院許可・退院後の生活指導

Dialogue
A = Doctor B = Patient

Audio 2-21

Permission to leave the hospital

A: Good morning. I have some good news.
B: Really? Discharge time?
A: Exactly.
B: That's wonderful!
A: Your test results finally came back clear!
B: So when can I go home?
A: Actually, you can go home tomorrow morning.
B: That's a relief!
A: ① What are you looking forward to?
B: I am excited about getting back to my daily routine.
A Well, before you pack your things, we need to talk about a few things.
B: Yes, of course.
A: Because you are recovering from surgery, you need to come see me every Wednesday and you will also have to continue coming to rehab at least two times a week.
B: Okay, no problem. I'll continue the rehab with my PT.
A: Do you have any other questions?
B: Yes, what kind of exercise can I do?
A: ② As far as exercise goes, please do gentle, simple activities like

walking or swimming only.
B: Okay. May I start packing my things?
A: Yes, you may.

Vocabulary Check Audio 2-22

(1)〜(6) に合う語義をそれぞれ (a)〜(f) から選びなさい。

(1) discharge   ( )   (2) exactly   ( )
(3) exercise   ( )   (4) gentle   ( )
(5) pack   ( )   (6) routine   ( )

(a) 運動 (b) 退院 (c) 日課 (d) 穏やかな (e) そのとおりです (f) 荷造りする

Useful Expressions Audio 2-23

❶ Dialogue 中の下線部①の表現を参照し、音声を聴いて、(　) を埋めましょう。

(1) またすぐにあなたに会えるのを楽しみにしています。
　　I'm looking forward (　) (　) (　) again soon.

(2) 休暇が楽しみです。友人とフィレンツェに行くんです。
　　I'm looking forward (　) (　) (　). I'm going to Florence with my friend.

❷ Dialogue 中の下線部②の表現を参照し、音声を聴いて、(　) を埋めましょう。

(1) それに関しては、あとで彼女と話した方がいい。
　　As far as (　) (　), we'd better talk about it with her later.

(2) それに関して言うと、我々はもっと慎重になるべきだ。
　　As far as (　) (　) concerned, we have to be more careful.

(3) 私に関して言えば、その件に関しては全く気にしていません。
　　As far as (　) (　) (　), I don't care about that at all.

Discharge Guidance

🔊 Audio 2-24

A = Nurse   B = Patient   C = Nutritionist

A: Good morning, Mr. Cook. Are you all packed and ready to go?
B: Yes, I am.
A: Before you leave, do you have any questions about your medications?
B: No, I don't. The pharmacist explained things very clearly.
A: Well, please contact us if anything comes up.
B: Okay.
A: ① <u>Our nutritionist will come talk to you soon.</u> This is a necessary discharge procedure, so please wait here a little while.

Ten minutes later

C: Good morning, Mr. Cook. I'm Janice, your nutritionist.
B: Good morning, Janice. You wanted to talk to me about my diet and lifestyle?
C: Yes, that's right. I'd like to ask you a few questions.
B: Okay. Go ahead.
C: To begin with, how many meals do you eat a day?
B: I always try to eat three meals a day, but….
C: So, your eating schedule is the same most days?
B: Hmmm, recently I often skipped breakfast and had dinner late at night after getting home.
C: I see. Do you usually eat snacks?
B: I usually eat a snack in the afternoon.
C: Okay. After you leave here, you should try to have a balanced-diet. And please don't eat spicy food for a while. ② <u>You have to be careful about what you eat.</u> ③ <u>And it's really important to eat three meals daily.</u> Well-regulated eating habits can lead to good health.
B: I see. I'll try to eat healthy food.
C: What about alcohol? How often do you drink?
B: I like alcohol and I drink it once a week.
C: That's good, but you can't drink until your doctor gives you permission. What about cigarettes? Do you smoke?
B: No, I don't.
C: Okay, great. You know, smoking can seriously damage our health. Do you do any sports or exercise regularly?
B: Well, I usually jog on weekends.
C: Thank you. Right, this is the last question. Do you have any history

of illness or allergies?
B: I'm allergic to cheese.
C: Okay, that's all. Thank you.

Vocabulary Check
Audio 2-25

(1) ～ (10) に合う語義をそれぞれ (a) ～ (j) から選びなさい。

(1) a little while ( )   (2) contact ( )
(3) damage ( )   (4) diet ( )
(5) habit ( )   (6) nutritionist ( )
(7) permission ( )   (8) regularly ( )
(9) snack ( )   (10) skip ( )

(a) 栄養士　(b) 許可　(c) 軽食　(d) 習慣　(e) 食事　(f) 規則正しく
(g) しばらく　(h) 害を与える　(i) 抜く　(j) 連絡する

Useful Expressions

❶ Dialogue 中の下線部①の表現を参照し、音声を聴いて、リピートしましょう。　Audio 2-26

★ come to do や come and do は「〜をしに来る」という表現ですが、and は省略されることがあります。

(1) If I feel pain in a week, I'll come see you again.
（もし一週間後痛むようでしたら、また受診しに来ます。）

(2) Would you like to come see us next Sunday?（今度の日曜日、遊びに来ませんか。）

(3) Will you come have dinner with me?（夕食を食べにいらっしゃいませんか。）

(4) We'll go see a movie tomorrow.（明日映画を見に行きます。）

❷ Dialogue 中の下線部②の表現を参照し、音声を聴いて、(　) を埋めましょう。　Audio 2-27

(1) すみませんが、これは私が注文した物ではありません。
Excuse me, but this is not (　　) (　) (　　).

(2) これは私が本当にほしいものです。
This is (　　) (　) really (　　).

(3) 私の言いたいことが分かりますか？
Do you understand (　　) (　) (　)?

(4) 彼は私がしたことを聞いて怒った。
He got angry when he heard (　) (　) (　) (　　).

❸ Dialogue 中の下線部③の表現を使い、< >内の語を並べ替えて、英文を完成させましょう。ただし、文頭に来る語も小文字で示しています。

(1) 今月末までにレポートを仕上げるのは無理だ。
< my / me / by / finish / it / for / is / impossible / paper / to> the end of the month.

_____

_____

(2) この医療機器の使い方を理解するのは難しかった。
< was / understand / use / it / difficult / me / how / for / to / to> this medical device.

_____

_____

看護は文化

　「看護は文化」です。日本で勉強する看護は日本の文化に即した看護です。出産、育児、看取りの方法などは民族によって異なります。異文化体験をすることは、日本の文化を再認識することにもなります。外国に行き、人と交流して彼らの生き方などに触れることは視野を広げることになります。世界には、内戦や感染症などで助けを必要としている人々がたくさんいます。日本の青年海外協力隊、国連、NGO（民間団体）など皆さんを必要としている国際協力の組織があります。勇気をもって国際協力にも挑戦して欲しいと思います。国際協力は、助けを必要としている人々のために働くことですが、実は彼らからそれ以上のものを受けていることに気づくことでしょう。これが国際協力の醍醐味です。

Unit 14 退院

Dialogue

A = Doctor (Dr. Clifford)   B = Patient (Mr. Cook)

A: Mr. Cook, you look good and you are leaving here soon.
B: Yup… I'm ready to go home, Doctor. I really appreciate what you've done for me.
A: My pleasure.
B: Now I realize the importance of good health.
A: Good. ① We don't appreciate good health until we lose it.
B: Yes, you're right.
A: You should have regular habits, have balanced meals, get moderate exercise and sleep well. It's also important to relieve stress.
B: I really understand.
A: ② After leaving here, please remember to take the medicine which I prescribed. And you need to come see me once a week until the end of this month, okay? I also recommend that you get a medical check-up once a year.
B: Yes, I will. I'll take care of myself and do my best to stay healthy.
A: I'm glad to hear that. Please take care.

A = Doctor (Dr. Jones)　B = Patient (Jane)

A: You look happy, Jane. I'm glad you recovered from the injury.
B: Thank you, Dr. Jones. ③At first I was really depressed, but thanks to all the staff, I could concentrate on getting better. I'm happy that I received good care here. ④Without your encouragement, I could not have gotten better.
A: We are really happy to see our patients get better and smile again.
B: I will never forget all you have done for me. Thank you very much.
A: It's my pleasure.

Vocabulary Check　　Audio 2-29

(1)～(4) に合う語義をそれぞれ (a)～(d) から選びなさい。

(1) appreciate　　(　)　　(2) concentrate　　(　)
(3) encouragement　(　)　　(4) moderate　　(　)

(a) 適度の　　(b) 励まし　　(c) 感謝する、その価値を認める　　(d) 専念する

Useful Expressions

❶ Dialogue 中の下線部①の表現を参照し、以下の英文を日本語に訳しましょう。

★ not ～ until… は、「…してはじめて～する」と訳をします。

(1) Steve didn't come until the class was almost over.

_____

(2) I couldn't understand what my father had said until I failed.

_____

❷ Dialogue 中の下線部②の表現を参照し、(　) に適切な関係代名詞を書きましょう。

(1)「昨日あなたが会ったお医者さんはリサのお母さんよ。」
　「え、そうなの？クリフォード先生がリサのお母さんなの？知らなかったよ。」
　"The doctor (　　　) you met yesterday is Lisa's mother."
　"Oh, really? Dr. Clifford is her mother? I didn't know that."

(2) 私たちが見たあの映画はとても面白かった。
　The movie (　　　) we watched was really interesting.

(3) ケンと話しているあの女性を知っていますか。
Do you know the woman (　　　) is talking with Ken?

(4) すみませんが、ジェーン・スミスという名前の患者さんがいる部屋を教えてくれませんか。
Excuse me, could you tell me which room the patient (　　　) name is Jane Smith is in?

❸ Dialogue 中の下線部③の表現を参照し、音声を聴いて、(　) を埋めましょう。 Audio 2-30

(1) あなたのアドバイスのおかげで、健康でいられます。
Thanks to your (　　　), I can stay (　　　).

(2) あなたの温かいおもてなしのおかげで、ここで素晴らしい時間を過ごせました。
Thanks to your (　　　), I had a wonderful time here.

❹ Dialogue 中の下線部④の表現を参照し、音声を聴いて、(　) を埋めましょう。 Audio 2-31

★ without~「~がなければ、~がなかったならば」は、主節が仮定法過去・仮定法過去完了になります。それぞれ If it were not for ~、If it had not been for ~ に置き換えることが可能です。

(1) もしあなたがいなければ、彼らは途方にくれているでしょう。
Without you, they (　　　) (　　) at a loss.

(2) あなたの助けがなかったならば、私はこのプロジェクトを終わらせることはできなかったでしょう。
Without your help, I could not (　　　) (　　) this project.

 感謝の表現　　　　　　　　　　　　　　　　　　　　　　Audio 2-32

音声を聴いて、リピートしましょう。

(1) "Thanks for your help." "No problem."
（「手伝ってくれてありがとう。」「どういたしまして。」）

(2) "Thank you for helping me with my assignment." "My pleasure."
（「宿題を手伝ってくれて、ありがとう。」「どういたしまして。」）

(3) "Thank you so much for what you have done for me." "You're welcome."
（「あなたが私のためにしてくださったことに感謝します。」「どういたしまして。」）

(4) "Thank you very much. That was kind of you." "Don't mention it."
（「どうもありがとうございました。ご親切さま。」「どういたしまして。」）

(5) "I really appreciate your kindness." "Not at all."
（「ご親切にしていただき、ありがとうございます。」「どういたしまして。」）

AED（自動体外式除細動器）と心肺蘇生法

Audio 2-33

A = Steve   B = Lisa

A: Hi, Lisa. How are you doing?
B: Steve! I've just been to a workshop about an AED.
A: Really? I didn't know that.
B: My mom told me to attend to learn to how to use an AED. She was also there as an instructor. There were many nurses and some nursing students there like me.
A: Sounds good.
B: If you are interested, there will be another workshop next Friday.
A: Thank you for the information.
B: Oh, I have one more handout about the procedure. You can have it.
A: Thanks. Why don't you show me how to use it with this?
B: Why not?

❶ Dialogue を聴いて、リピートしましょう。

❷ 以下の AED の説明の①〜⑩の部分を日本語に訳してみましょう。

Automated External Defibrillator & Cardio Pulmonary Resuscitation
AED（自動体外式除細動器）と心肺蘇生法

1. If you see a person who has fallen down on the ground, you need to say "Are you all right?" or "Can you hear me?" loudly while patting his/her shoulder.
   もし誰かが倒れているのを発見したら、その人の肩を（①　　　　）ながら大きな声で「大丈夫ですか？」や「聞こえますか？」と声をかける。

2. If there is no response, you have to ask someone for help saying, "Somebody, come quickly!" And then you need to get them to call an ambulance and bring an AED right away.
   もし反応がなかったら、「誰か来てください！」と大声で助けを求め、（②　　　　）と AED 搬送を依頼する。

3. You have to check his/her breathing while watching the movement of his/her chest and abdomen.
   （③　　　　）と（④　　　　）の動きを見て、（⑤　　　　）を確認する。

4. If he/she isn't breathing, you need to carry out chest compression [cardio pulmonary resuscitation] by pressing the breastbones strongly with your palms. You should carry it out continuously for thirty repetitions at a rate of 100 times per minute.
   呼吸がなかったら、（⑥　　　　）を使って胸骨の上を強く押すことで、胸骨圧迫（chest compression）を行う。少なくとも 1 分間に 100 回のテンポで、30 回連続で圧迫する。

5. When the AED arrives, you need to turn it on.
   AEDが到着したら、(⑦　　　　　　)。

6. You need to follow the directions of the AED and put the electrode pads on the breast. Then you must tell the people to stay away.
   AEDの指示に従い、電極パッドを胸に貼る。他の人は(⑧　　　　　　)ように指示を与える。

7. The AED indicates whether an electric shock is necessary or not.
   電気ショックが必要かどうかの判断はAEDが行う。

8. When it is necessary to give an electric shock, you must check that no one is touching him/her and then push the button according to the instructions. After this you must continue to follow the directions.
   電気ショックが必要なときは、AEDの指示に従って、(⑨　　　　　　)を確認し、通電ボタンを押す。この後も引き続きAEDの指示に(⑩　　　　　　)。

Glossary

A

abdomen	[名]腹部		appendix	[名]虫垂
abdominal	[形]腹部の		appetite	[名]食欲
aboard	[副]搭乗して		apply	[動](薬を)塗る
accept	[動]受け入れる、支払いに応じる		apply for ~	[動]~を申し込む
accident	[名]事故		appointment	[名]約束、予約
according to ~	~によると		appreciate	[動]正しく理解する、感謝する
ache	[名]痛み／[動]痛む		appropriately	[副]ふさわしく、適切に
a couple of ~	[形]2、3の、幾つかの		arcade	[名]アーケード
activity	[名]活動		arm	[名]腕
actually	[副]実際に		armpit	[名]脇の下
acute	[形]激しい、急性の		around	[前]~の周りに／[副]およそ、約
add	[動]加える、付け足す		arrive	[名]到着する
administer	[動]投与する		arrow	[名]矢印
admission	[名]入場、入院		article	[名]記事
advice	[名]助言、忠告		as far as that goes [that is concerned] それに関して言えば	
advise	[動]勧める、助言する		ask	[動]尋ねる、頼む
a few	[形]少しの		aspirin	[名]アスピリン
afraid	[形]残念に思って		assignment	[名]宿題、課題
ahead	[副]前に		assist	[動]助ける、手伝う
aircraft	[名]航空機		asthma	[名]喘息
aisle	[名]通路		as usual	[副]いつものように
alcohol	[名]アルコール、酒		at a loss	[形]困って、途方に暮れて
all day long	[副]一日中		at first	[副]最初は
allergic	[形]アレルギーの		at least	[副]少なくとも
allergy	[名]アレルギー		atmosphere	[名]雰囲気
along	[前]~に沿って		attend	[動]参加する、出席する
ambulance	[名]救急車		available	[形]入手できる、利用できる
amount	[名]量		avoid	[動]避ける
amusement park	[名]遊園地		awhile	[副]しばらく
and so on	[副]~など			
ankle	[名]足首			

B

annoy	[動]いらだたせる、悩ます
another	[形]もう一つの、別の
antibiotic	[名]抗生物質
anus	[名]肛門
anything else	[名]他に何か
anytime	[副]いつでも
anyway	[副]いずれにしても、ともかく
apologize	[動]謝罪する
appendicitis	[名]虫垂炎

back	[名]背中、腰
badly	[副]とても、ひどく
baggage	[名]手荷物
bake	[動]焼く
balanced	[形]バランスのとれた
Band-Aid	[名]バンドエイド、絆創膏
bargain	[名]お買い得品、割引き値
bathroom	[名]浴室、トイレ
be able to do	~することができる

beach	[名]浜辺
bed bath	[名]清拭
bee	[名]蜂
before	[副]以前に
begin	[動]始める
better	[形]good, well の比較級
bill	[名]勘定、紙幣
blanket	[名]毛布
bleed	[動]出血する
block	[名]区画
blood	[名]血液
blood pressure	[名]血圧
boarding pass	[名]搭乗券
body	[名]体
boring	[形]うんざりさせる、退屈な
boss	[名]上司
both	[形]両方の
bound for ~	[形]～行きの
break	[名]休憩／[動]骨折する、(小銭に)崩す、壊す
breast	[名]胸、胸部
breastbone	[名]胸骨
breast-feed	[動]母乳で育てる
breath	[名]息、呼吸
breathe	[動]呼吸する
bring	[動]持ってくる
bronchi	[名]bronchus「気管支」の複数
burn	[名]火傷／[動]やけどさせる
busy	[形]忙しい
by oneself	[副]一人で、独力で
by the way	ところで

C

calf	[名]ふくらはぎ
call	[名]電話の呼び出し、通話／[動]呼ぶ、電話をかける
cancel	[動]取り消す
cancer	[名]癌
capsule	[名]カプセル
careful	[形]慎重な、用心深い
carry-on bag	[名]機内持ち込み荷物
carry out	[動]実行する
cash	[名]現金　[動]現金に換える
cast	[名]ギプス
catch	[動](病気などに)かかる、感染する、移される
cause	[動]引き起こす
cavity	[名]虫歯
cell	[名]細胞
cell phone	[名]携帯電話
Celsius	[名]摂氏度
centigrade	[名]摂氏度、百分度
certainly	[副]かしこまりました。承知しました。
change	[名]釣り銭、小銭／[動]変更する、着替えさせる、両替する
chart	[名]カルテ、図表
chat	[動]おしゃべりをする
check	[動]検査する、預ける、
check-in	[名](ホテル、空港での)チェックイン
checkup	[名]検査、健康診断
chest	[名]胸、胸部
chew	[動]噛み砕く
childhood	[名]子供時代
chill	[名]悪寒、寒気
chilly	[形]ぞくぞくする、寒気がする
circle	[動]丸で囲む
circulation	[名]循環
class	[名]授業
clean	[動]きれいにする、清潔にする
clear	[動]片付ける
climb	[動]登る
clinic	[名]医院
clock	[名]時計
close	[動]閉める
close to ~	[副]～のすぐ近くに
clothes	[名]衣服
cold	[名]風邪／[形]寒い、冷たい
come out	[動]抜ける、はずれる
commission	[名]手数料
completely	[副]完全に、十分に、すっかり、徹底的に、全く
computer	[名]コンピューター、パソコン
concentrate on ~	[動]～に集中する
concern	[名]懸念、心配／[動]心配させる
concert	[名]コンサート
condition	[名]健康状態、体調
conference	[名]会議
connecting	[形]乗り継ぎの
constantly	[副]絶えず

consult	[動] 相談する、意見を求める	difficult	[形] 難しい
contact	[動] 連絡する	difficulty	[名] 困難、問題
continue	[動] 続ける	digestion	[名] 消化
continuously	[副] 連続的に	dime	[名] 10セント硬貨
convention	[名] 大会、会議	direction	[名] 道順、指示
conversation	[名] 会話	discharge	[名] 退院
cook	[動] 料理をする	discuss	[動] 話し合う
corporation	[名] 株式会社、企業	disease	[名] 病気
correct	[形] 正しい、正確な	dizzy	[名] 目まいがする
cost	[動]（費用が）かかる	document	[名] 書類
cotton ball	[名] 脱脂綿	draft beer	[名] 生ビール
counter	[名] カウンター、窓口	dressing	[名] 包帯、手当て用品
cough	[名] 咳／[動] 咳をする	drip	[名] 点滴
cramp	[動] 痙攣を起こす	drive	[動] 車を運転する
crutch	[名] 松葉杖	drowsy	[形] うとうとしている、眠い
customs	[名] 税関	drug	[名] 薬
customs form	[名] 税関申告書	duodenal	[形] 十二指腸の
cut	[動] 切る	dull	[形] 鈍い
		during	[前] 〜の間に

D

E

daily	[副] 毎日	ease	[動] 和らげる
damage	[動] 害を与える	electrode	[形] 電極
date	[名] 日、日付	emergency	[名] 緊急事態、急患／[形] 緊急の
daughter	[名] 娘	encouragement	[名] 激励
decide	[動] 決める	end	[名] 突き当たり
declare	[動] 申告する	energetic	[形] エネルギッシュな、元気な
definitely	[副] 確かに、はっきりと、全くその通り	entrance	[名] 入口、玄関
degree	[名] 度	equipment	[名] 機器、備品
delay	[動] 遅らせる、延ばす	especially	[副] 特に、とりわけ
delicious	[形] とても美味しい	exactly	[副] 正確に、厳密に、そのとおり
dental	[形] 歯科の	examination	[名] 診察、検査、試験
dentist	[名] 歯科医	exercise	[名] 運動／[動] 運動をする
depart	[動] 出発する	Excellent.	たいへんけっこうです。
department	[名] 部門、科	excessive	[形] 過度の
departure	[名] 出発	excited	[形] 興奮した
depress	[動] 意気消沈させる、憂鬱にさせる	exciting	[形] わくわくさせる
dessert	[名] デザート	exchange	[名] 為替／[動] 交換する
develop	[動] 発達させる、開発する	exchange rate	[名] 為替レート
device	[名] 装置、機器	exhibit	[名] 展覧会
diabetes	[名] 糖尿病	exit	[名] 出口
diagnose	[動] 診断する	expect	[動] 期待する、予期する
diarrhea	[名] 下痢	expensive	[形] 高価な
dictionary	[名] 辞書	explain	[動] 説明する
diet	[名] 食事	express	[動] 表現する、述べる
different	[形] 異なる、違う		

extra	[形] 余分の	form	[名] 申し込み用紙
extremely	[副] 極度に、とても	formality	[名] 正規の手続き
eye	[名] 目	forward	[副] 前方へ
eye drop	[名] 目薬	freely	[副] 自由に
everything	[名] 全てのもの	French fries	[名] フライドポテト
		fridge = refrigerator	[名] 冷蔵庫

F

		from now on	[副] 今後
Fahrenheit	[名] 華氏	full	[形] 満員の
fail	[動] 失敗する	fully	[副] 十分に、完全に
fall down	[動] 倒れる、転倒する		
fantastic	[形] すばらしい		

G

far	[形] 遠い	game	[名] 試合
fare	[名] 運賃	gargle	[動] うがいをする
fasten	[動] しっかり固定する	gastroscope	[名] 胃カメラ
fee	[名] 料金	gastroscopy	[名] 胃カメラ検査
feel	[動] 感じる	gate	[名] (空港の) 搭乗口、ゲート
feeling	[名] 感情、気持ち	gentle	[形] 穏やかな
feel like ~ing	[動] ~したい気分だ	gently	[副] 穏やかに、静かに、優しく
feet	[名] foot の複数形	get	[動] ~の状態になる
foot	[名] 足	get lost	[動] 迷う
fever	[名] 熱	get out of ~	[動] ~から降りる
feverish	[形] 熱っぽい	get started	[動] 始める
file	[名] ファイル	get to ~	[動] ~に到着する
fill	[動] 調剤する	get to work	[動] 仕事に取りかかる
filling	[名] 詰め物	give	[動] 与える
fill out	[動] 必要事項を記入する	give it a try	[動] ためにやってみる
final	[形] 最後の	give up	[動] やめる
finally	[副] ついに、やっと	go out	[動] 外出する
find	[動] 見つける、~だと分かる	go over ~	[動] ~を調べる
fine	[形] 元気な、すばらしい、けっこうな	go through	[動] (苦しみ、治療などを) 受ける
finger	[名] (手の) 指	get together	[動] 集まる
finish	[動] 終える	go well	[動] うまくいく
fire	[名] 火事	gown	[名] 上衣、室内着
first of all	[副] まず第一に	gradually	[副] 徐々に
fit	[形] 健康で、体調が良い	griping	[形] きりきり痛む、差し込むような、激しい
flight	[名] 便、フライト	gum	[名] 歯茎
floor	[名] 階		
floss	[名] 糸、デンタルフロス		
flu	[名] インフルエンザ		

H

fly direct to~	[動] 直行便で~へ行く	habit	[名] 習慣
focus	[動] 焦点を合わせる	had better do	[動] ~すべきである
follow	[動] 従う	hair	[名] 髪、体毛
for a while	[副] しばらくの間	hall	[名] 玄関、廊下
forecast	[名] 予報	hand	[名] 手／[動] 手渡す
forget	[動] 忘れる	handout	[名] プリント、配布資料

happen	[動]起こる、生じる		inside	[副]内側に
happy	[形]うれしい、幸せな		instead	[副]その代りに
hard	[副]懸命に、熱心に		instruction	[名]指示
hardly	[副]ほとんど〜ない		instructor	[名]指導者
hay fever	[名]花粉症		instrument	[名]道具、器具
headache	[名]頭痛		insurance	[名]保険
heal	[動]治る、癒える		international	[形]国際的な
health	[名]健康		interesting	[形]面白い
healthy	[形]健康的な、健康に良い		interview	[名]面接
hear	[動]聞こえる、聞く		in the meantime	[副]その合間に
heart	[名]心臓		in time	[副]間に合って
heel	[名]かかと		intramuscular	[形]筋肉内の
help	[名]助け／[動]手伝う		invite	[名]招待
history	[名]病歴、既往歴		itchy	[形]かゆい
hold	[動]つかむ		IV drip = intravenous drip	
Hold on.	[動](電話を)切らずにお待ちください。			[名]点滴、静脈注射
hospital	[名]病院			
hospitality	[名]親切なおもてなし、歓待		**J**	
hospitalization	[名]入院		join	[動]参加する、加わる
hour	[名]1時間		jog	[動]ジョギングする
however	[副]しかしながら		just in case	[副]万一の場合に備えて
hungry	[形]空腹の			
hurt	[動]痛む、怪我をさせる		**K**	
husband	[名]夫		kind	[名]種類／[形]親切な
hygienist	[名]衛生技師		kindness	[名]親切、親切な行為
			knife	[名]ナイフ、包丁
I			know	[動]知っている
ID	[名]身分証明書			
ill	[形]病気の、気分が悪い		**L**	
illness	[名]病気		label	[名]ラベル
important	[形]重要な		land	[動]着陸する
impossible	[形]不可能な、無理な		last name	[名]苗字
in advance	[副]前もって、事前に		lately	[副]最近
include	[動]含む		later	[副]後で
inconvenience	[名]不便、迷惑		lead	[動]至る
infect	[動]伝染する、感染する		learn to do	[動]〜できるようになる
infectious	[形]伝染性の、感染性の		leave	[動]去る
inflame	[動]炎症を起こす		left	[名]左側／[副]左に
inflammation	[名]炎症		leg	[名]脚
information	[名]情報		library	[名]図書館
in front of ~	[副]〜の前に		lie down	[動]横になる
inhaler	[名]吸入器		line	[名]電話線
injection	[名]注射		liquid	[形]液体の
injury	[名]怪我		lobby	[名]ロビー
in particular	[副]特に、とりわけ		look	[動]〜のように見える

look forward to ~	[動]～を楽しみに待つ		negatively	[副]悲観的に、悪い方に
loosen up	[動]肩の力を抜く		nervous	[形]緊張して、不安な
lose	[動]失う		next	[名]次の人
loudly	[副]大声で		next to ~	[副]～の隣の
lozenge	[名]薬用ドロップ		nicely	[副]上手く
luggage	[名]手荷物		nickel	[名]5セント硬貨
lung	[名]肺		noon	[名]正午
			normal	[形]正常な、通常の
			normally	[副]正常に、普通は
			notice	[動]気付く
			numb	[形]無感覚な、麻痺した、しびれた
			numbness	[名]無感覚
			nurse	[名]看護師
			nutritionist	[名]栄養士

M

ma'am	[名]（女性への呼びかけ）あなた
machine	[名]機械
machinery	[名]機械、機器
main	[形]主要な、中心となる
make sure to do	[動]必ず～するようにする
malignant	[名]悪性
mall	[名]ショッピングセンター
manageable	[形]扱いやすい、ほどほどの
massage	[名]マッサージ／[動]マッサージする
matter	[名]問題／[動]重要である
maybe	[副]おそらく、たぶん
meal	[名]食事
mean	[動]意味する
measles	[名]はしか、麻疹
mechanical	[形]機械の
medical	[形]医療の、医学の
medication	[名]薬剤
medicine	[名]薬剤、医学
message	[名]伝言
mind	[動]嫌だと思う、気にする
minute	[名]分、ちょっとの間
miss	[動]見落とす
mistake	[名]誤り、間違い
moderate	[形]穏やかな、適度の
moment	[名]ちょっと、瞬間
monitor	[名]モニター、画面
month	[名]月、ひと月
move	[動]動く、動かす
movement	[名]動き
museum	[名]博物館
My pleasure.	どういたしまして。

O

occur	[動]生じる、起こる
ointment	[名]軟膏
once	[副]かつて、一度
one-way	[形]片道の
on schedule	[副]予定通りに
on time	[副]時間通りに、定刻に
opening	[名]空き
operate	[動]操作する、運転する
operating room	[名]手術室
operation	[名]手術
opportunity	[名]機会
opposite	[前]～の向かいに
order	[名]注文　[動]注文する
outside	[副]外に
over	[前]～しながら／[副]終わって、済んで
overdose	[名]過剰服用／[動]過量摂取する
overseas	[副]海外へ
overtime	[副]時間外に
overweight	[名]肥満／[形]重量超過の

N

nauseous	[形]吐き気のする
necessity	[名]必要性
neck	[名]首

P

pack	[動]荷造りする
pain	[名]苦痛、痛み／[動]痛む
painful	[形]痛い
palm	[名]手のひら
pan	[名]なべ
paper	[名]新聞、論文、レポート
parallel	[形]平行の
participate	[動]参加する

party	[名]一行、一団	problem	[名]問題
pass	[名]通行証／[動]合格する	procedure	[名]手順、手続き
passenger	[名]乗客	process	[名]過程、手順
past	[形]過去の	prohibit	[動]禁止する
pat	[動]軽くたたく	project	[名]計画、企画、事業
patient	[名]患者／[形]忍耐強い、我慢する	properly	[副]適切に、きちんと、正確に
pay	[動]支払う	provided	[形]備え付けの
penny	[名]1セント硬貨	PT = physical therapist	[名]理学療法士
per	[前]〜につき	purpose	[名]目的
perfect	[形]申し分のない	push	[動]押す
personal belongings	[名]所持品、私物	put	[動]置く
pharmacist	[名]薬剤師	put off	[動]延期する
pharmacy	[名]薬局	put on	[動]〜を身に付ける、着る
phlegm	[名]痰	put through	[動](電話を)つなぐ

Q

physical	[形]身体の	quarter	[名]4分の1、25セント硬貨
pick up	[動]迎えに行く、手に取る	question	[名]質問
piece	[名]一つ	questionnaire	[名]アンケート用紙、質問事項
pill	[名]丸薬、錠剤	quick	[形]素早い
pillow case	[名]枕カバー	quickly	[副]すぐに、急いで

R

place	[動]置く	rain	[動]雨が降る
plan	[名]計画	rainy	[形]雨の
please	[動]喜ばせる、好む	rash	[名]吹き出物、発疹
pneumonia	[名]肺炎	rate	[名]速度、ペース
point at ~	[動]〜を指し示す	reach	[名]届く範囲／[動]到着する
polish	[動]磨く	read	[動]読む
polyp	[名]ポリープ	ready	[形]用意が出来た
porter	[名]ポーター、ボーイ	receipt	[名]領収書
possible	[形]可能な	receive	[動]受ける
possibility	[名]可能性	receptionist	[名]受付係
powder	[名]粉薬	recommend	[動]勧める
practice	[動]練習する	reconfirm	[動]再確認する
pregnant	[形]妊娠している	recover	[動]回復する
preparation	[名]準備	reduce	[動]減少する、縮小する、弱める
prescribe	[動](薬を)処方する	refrain	[動]差し控える、我慢する
prescription	[名]処方箋、処方薬	registration	[名]登録
presentation	[名]口頭発表、プレゼンテーション	regular	[形]通常の、規則正しい、正常な
president	[名]社長	regularly	[副]規則正しく、定期的に
press	[動]押す	rehab = rehabilitation	[名]リハビリテーション
pretty	[副]かなり		
prevent	[動]防ぐ		
previous	[形]前の、以前の		
prior to~	[副]〜より前に		
probably	[副]おそらく	relax	[動]くつろぐ、リラックスする

relieve	[動] 取り除く、和らげる		shortly	[副] すぐに、まもなく
remember	[動] 覚えている		shot	[名] 注射
repetition	[名] 繰り返し、反復		show	[動] 示す、案内する
replace	[動] 取り替える、取って代わる		showing	[名] 上映
reschedule	[動] 予定を変更する		shuttle bus	[名] 近距離往復バス、シャトルバス
research	[名] 研究、調査		side effect	[名] (薬の) 副作用
reservation	[名] 予約		sightseeing	[名] 観光
reserve	[動] 予約する		sign	[名] 標識、看板
respiratory	[名] 呼吸の		signature	[名] 署名、サイン
response	[名] 反応、応答		simple	[形] 単純な
result	[名] 結果		single	[形] 一人用の
right	[名] 右側／[副] 右に		since	[前] 〜以来／[接] 〜して以来
right away	[副] すぐに、ただちに		sir	[名] (男性への呼びかけ) あなた
ring	[動] 鳴る、響く		sit up	[動] 起き上がる
rinse	[動] ゆすぐ、すすぐ		skilled	[形] 上手な、熟練した、腕のいい
robe	[名] ローブ		skin	[名] 皮膚
roll up	[動] 巻き上げる		skip	[動] 飛ばす、省く、抜く
room	[名] 部屋、空間		sleep	[動] 眠る
round-trip	[形] 往復の		sleeve	[名] 袖
routine	[名] 日課		slight	[形] 少しの、わずかな
rub	[動] 擦り込む、こする		slowly	[副] ゆっくり
run	[動] 流す、出す		smile	[動] 微笑む
runny nose	[名] 鼻水		smoke	[動] タバコを吸う
			snack	[名] 軽食
			sneeze	[動] くしゃみをする

S

sad	[形] 悲しい		snore	[動] いびきをかく
safe	[名] 金庫／[形] 安全な		so far	[副] 今のところ
safety	[名] 安全		sometimes	[副] 時々
say	[動] 〜と書いてある		somewhere	[副] どこかで
scale	[名] はかり		sore	[形] 痛い
scary	[形] 恐ろしい		sorry	[形] すまなく思う、気の毒に思う
schedule	[名] 予定／[動] 〜を予定する		sound	[動] 〜のように聞こえる、〜のように思われる
seat	[名] 座席			
second	[名] 秒、ちょっとの間		spasm	[名] 痙攣、ひきつけ
see	[動] 見える、会う		speak	[動] 話す
seem	[動] 〜のように思われる		special	[名] 特別料理、おすすめ品／[形] 特別の
separately	[副] 別々に		spell	[動] 綴る
serious	[形] 深刻な、重大な		spend	[動] 過ごす、使う
serve	[動] 食事を出す		split	[動] 分配する
settle	[動] 置く、落ち着かせる、座らせる		spoonful	[名] スプーン一杯分
severe	[形] 厳しい、耐えがたい		sprain	[動] くじく、捻挫する
shake	[動] 振る		staff	[名] 職員
sharp	[形] 鋭い		stairs	[名] 階段
sheet	[名] シーツ		stand	[動] 立つ
shopper	[名] 買い物客		stand for 〜	[動] 〜を表す、〜の略である

stay	[名]滞在／[動]ある状態のままでいる、滞在する		throat	[名]喉
stay away	[動]離れている		throbbing	[形]ずきずきする
step	[動]歩いて進む		ticket	[名]チケット、切符
still	[形]じっとした／[副]まだ		time	[名]〜回、度
sting	[名]刺し傷／[動]ひりひり痛む		tip	[名]チップ
stomach	[名]胃		tired	[形]疲れた
stomachache	[名]腹痛、胃痛		tissue	[名]組織
stool	[名]スツール、足のせ台		to begin with	[副]まず最初に
stop	[名]停留所／[動]やめる		tolerable	[形]耐えられる、我慢できる
straight	[副]まっすぐに		tonight	[副]今夜は
stress	[名]ストレス、緊張		tonsil	[名]扁桃腺
stretcher	[名]ストレッチャー、担架		tooth	[名]歯
stung	[動]sting の過去分詞		to start with	[副]まずはじめに
subway	[名]地下鉄		touch	[動]触れる
suffer	[動]苦しむ		tough	[形]つらい、厳しい、困難な
support	[名]支え／[動]支える		towel	[名]タオル
suppository	[名]座薬		traffic	[名]交通、交通量
surgery	[名]外科、外科手術		traffic light	[名]信号機
station	[名]駅		treat	[名]おごり、おごる番／[動]おごる、治療する、手当てする
swallow	[動]飲み込む		treatment	[名]治療、治療法
swell	[動]膨らむ、腫れる		trust	[動]信頼する
swim	[動]泳ぐ		try on	[動]試着する
swollen	[動]swell の過去分詞		tumor	[名]腫瘍
symptom	[名]徴候、症状		turbulence	[名]乱気流
			turn	[動]曲がる
T			turn off	[動](電源を)切る、消す
tablet	[名]錠剤		turn out	[動]〜であることが判明する
take a shower	[動]シャワーを浴びる		twice	[副]2回
take a walk	[動]散歩する		twist	[動]ひねる、捻挫する、ねじる
take care of ~	[動]〜の世話をする、介護をする		typically	[副]典型的に
Take it easy.	[動]気を楽にして。			
take off	[動](服を)脱ぐ、(飛行機が)離陸する		**U**	
thanks to ~	[前]〜のおかげで		ulcer	[名]潰瘍
tartar	[名]歯石		umbrella	[名]傘
taxi stand	[名]タクシー乗り場		under	[前]〜の下に
teeth	[名]tooth の複数形		understand	[動]理解する
temperature	[名]温度、気温		unfortunately	[副]あいにく、残念ながら、不運にも
terrible	[形]ひどい		until	[前]〜まで(ずっと)／[接]〜するまで
terribly	[副]とても、ひどく		upset	[形]混乱した、落胆した
test	[名]検査			
thermometer	[名]体温計		**V**	
thin	[形]痩せた		vacancy	[名]空室、空席
think	[動]考える、思う		vacation	[名]休暇、休日
thorough	[形]完全な、徹底的な			

vaccination	[名]	予防接種、ワクチン接種
vending machine	[名]	自動販売機
via	[前]	～によって、～を経て
viral	[形]	ウィルスの
visit	[名]	訪問、見舞い／[動]訪問する、見舞う
volunteer	[名]	ボランティア
vomit	[動]	嘔吐する、吐く

W

wait	[動]	待つ
want	[動]	ほしい
want to do	[動]	～したいと思う
warmly	[副]	親切に、温かく、心を込めて
warmth	[名]	温かさ
wash	[動]	洗う
watch	[動]	見る
way	[名]	道、方向、方法
weak	[形]	弱い、無力な
wear	[動]	着ている、身に付けている
weather	[名]	天候
weekend	[名]	週末
weight	[名]	重さ、体重
what's called = so-called		いわゆる
wheel chair	[名]	車いす
whenever	[接]	～するときはいつでも
while	[接]	～している間に
wide	[副]	十分に開いて
wife	[名]	妻
wisdom tooth	[名]	親知らず
wipe	[動]	拭く
without	[前]	～がなければ、～がなかったならば
wonder	[動]	～かなと思う
work on ~	[動]	～に取り組む
workshop	[名]	セミナー、講習会、勉強会
worry	[動]	心配する、気にする
worse	[形]	bad, ill の比較級
wound	[名]	傷
wrong	[形]	具合が悪い、誤っている

X

x-ray	[名]	レントゲン写真

Y

yawn	[動]	あくびをする
yep (yup)	[副]	うん、そうだね

Z

zipcode	[名]	郵便番号

医療用語英日対照表 (五十音順)

院内施設名称

🔊 Audio 2-34

育児室	nursery
受付	information / reception
会計	cashier
回復室	recovery room
外来	outpatient department
救急救命室	emergency room
結核病棟	tuberculosis ward
検査室	lab / laboratory
個室	private room
集中治療室(ICU)	intensive care unit
手術室	operating room
食堂	dining room
処置室	treatment room
診察室	examining room
伝染病棟	contagious disease ward
ナースステーション	nurses' station
入院受付	admission
病棟	ward
分娩室	delivery room
待合室	waiting room
薬局	pharmacy
リハビリ施設	rehabilitation center
レントゲン室	x-ray room

hospital staff (病院職員)

🔊 Audio 2-35

医師	doctor / physician
医療検査技師	lab technician / medical technologist
院長	director
受付係	receptionist
栄養士	dietician / nutritionist
看護師	nurse
患者	patient
管理者	administrator
技師	technical expert
救急救命士 (EMT)	emergency medical technician
雑役係	orderly
歯科衛生士	dental hygienist
歯科助手	dental assistant
上級救急救命士	paramedic
入院受付係	admissions clerk
薬剤師	pharmacist
理学療法士	physical therapist
療法士	therapist

medical specialists (専門医)

🔊 Audio 2-36

医学生	medical student
一般開業医	general practitioner

medical specialists (専門医)

眼科医	ophthalmologist
形成外科医	plastic surgeon
外科医	surgeon
研修医	intern
産科医	obstetrician
歯科医	dentist
耳鼻科医	otolaryngologist
小児科医	pediatrician
神経科医	neurologist
心臓専門医/循環器科医	cardiologist
整形外科医	orthopedist
精神科医	psychiatrist
当直医	doctors on duty
内科医	internist
泌尿器科医	urologist
皮膚科医	dermatologist
婦人科医	gynecologist
放射線科医	radiologist
麻酔科医	anesthesiologist
臨床心理士	psychologist

departments (科)

心療内科	psychosomatic medicine
整形外科	orthopedics
精神科	psychiatry
内科	internal medicine
泌尿器科	urology
皮膚科	dermatology
婦人科	gynecology
放射線科	radiology
麻酔科	anesthetics

nursing staff (看護職員)

Audio 2-38

看護学生	student nurse
看護師長	head nurse
正看護師	registered nurse
准看護師	licensed practical nurse
助産師	obstetric nurse
認定看護助手	certified nursing assistant

departments (科)

Audio 2-37

眼科	ophthalmology
形成外科	plastic surgery
外科	surgery
産科	obstetrics
歯科	dentistry
耳鼻咽喉科	otolaryngology / ENT
循環器科	cardiology
小児科	pediatrics
神経科	neurology

薬の種類・関連語

Audio 2-39

アスピリン	aspirin
カプセル	capsule
丸薬	pill
薬の過剰摂取	overdosage
抗生物質	antibiotics
粉薬	powder
湿布	poultice

薬の種類・関連語

市販薬	over-the-counter medication
使用期限	expiration date
錠剤	tablet
処方箋	prescription
処方薬	prescription medication
制酸剤	antacid
咳止めシロップ	cough syrup
喘息の吸入器	inhaler
脱脂綿	absorbent cotton
鎮痛剤	pain killer
軟膏	ointment / salve
ビタミン剤	vitamins
服用量	dosage
目薬	eye drops
薬用ドロップ	throat lozenges

器具

診察台	examination table
心電図	electrocardiogram
接着包帯ばんそうこう	adhesive bandage
体温計	thermometer
担架	stretcher
注射器	syringe
聴診器	stethoscope
杖	cane
点滴	intravenous drip / IV drip
氷嚢	ice pack
ピンセット	tweezers
歩行器	walker
松葉杖	crutch

器具

Audio 2-40

温熱パッド	heating pad
ガーゼ	gauze
ギプス	cast
車いす	wheelchair
外科用メス	scalpel
血圧測定器	blood pressure monitor
差し込み便器、おまる	bedpan
三角巾	sling
手術台	operating table

処置、治療法、検査法

Audio 2-41

MRI	magnetic resonance imaging
血液検査	blood test
血管造影法	angiograhpy
CT	computerized tomography
心臓カテーテル	cardiac catheterization
陣痛促進	induction of labor
心電図検査	electrocardiography
切開	incision
切除	excision
切断	amputation
超音波検査	ultrasonography

処置、治療法、検査法

聴診	auscultation
帝王切開	Cesarean section
透視検査法	fluoroscopy
内視鏡検査	endoscopy
尿検査	urine test / urine sample
妊娠中絶	abortion
バリウム	barium meal
病理解剖	autopsy
輸血	blood transfusion
レーザー手術	laser surgery
レントゲン検査	x-ray examination

body parts (outside)

Audio 2-42

顎	jaw
顎先、下顎	chin
顎鬚	beard
脚	leg
足	foot / feet
足首	ankle
足の裏	sole
足の甲	instep
腕	arm
親指	thumb
顔	face
かかと	heal
肩	shoulder(s)
髪の毛	hair
胸部	chest

body parts (outside)

薬指（手）	the ring [third] finger
口	mouth
口髭	mustache
唇	lip(s)
首	neck
肩甲骨	shoulder blade(s)
腰	lower back
腰のくびれ	waist
腰回り	hip
小鼻、鼻孔	nostril
小指（手）	the little [fourth] finger / the pinkie
鎖骨	collarbone / clavicle
舌	tongue
上腕	upper arm
すね	shin
背中	back
前腕	forearm
大腿部	thigh
つま先、足の指	toe
手	hand
手のひら、掌	palm
手首	wrist
臀部	buttocks
頭部	head
中指（手）	the middle [second] finger
歯	tooth / teeth
歯茎	gums
鼻	nose
膝	lap

body parts (outside)

膝頭	knee
肘	elbow
額	forehead
人差し指（手）	the index [first] finger
腹部	abdomen / belly
ふくらはぎ	calf
へそ	navel / umbilicus
頬	cheak
まつ毛	eyelash(es)
瞼	eyelid
眉	eyebrow
耳	ear
胸、乳房	breast
目	eye
指	finger
脇の下	armpit

body parts (inside)

膵臓	pancreas
脊髄	spinal cord
脊柱	spinal column
胆嚢	gallbladder
腸	intestines
動脈	artery
脳	brain
喉	throat
肺	lung(s)
皮膚	skin
扁桃腺	tonsils
膀胱	bladder
骨	bone
肋骨	rib

body parts (inside)

胃	stomach 　Audio 2-43
関節	joint
肝臓	liver
気管	windpipe
筋肉	muscle
血管	blood vessel
子宮	uterine
静脈	vein
食道	esophagus
心臓	heart
腎臓	kidney (s)

symptoms（病気の症状）

Audio 2-44

アトピー性皮膚炎	eczema
痣	birthmark
アルコール依存症	alcoholism
アルツハイマー病	Alzheimer's disease
アレルギー	allergy
胃潰瘍	stomach ulcer
胃腸炎	gastroenteritis
いぼ	wart
インフルエンザ	flu
HIV(ヒト免疫不全ウィルス)	HIV(human immunodeficiency virus)
炎症	inflammation

symptoms (病気の症状)

黄疸	jaundice
嘔吐	vomitting
悪寒／寒気	chill
おたふく風邪	mumps
風邪	cold
肩の凝り	stiffness of shoulders
過食症	bulimia
花粉症	hay fever / pollen allergy
かゆみ	itchiness
癌	cancer
肝炎	hepatitis
眼球充血	red eyes
関節炎	arthritis
関節痛	joint pain
拒食症	sitophobia
くしゃみ	sneezing
けいれん／こむら返り	cramp
結核	TB(tuberculosis)
月経困難	dysmenorrhea
血尿	hematuria
下痢	diarrhea
倦怠感	lethargic
高血圧	high blood pressure / hypertension
呼吸困難	shortness of breath / dyspnea
コレラ	cholera
昏睡	coma
産褥	puerperium
痔	hemorrhoids
耳炎	ear infection
子宮外妊娠	ectopic pregnancy
子宮筋腫	uterine myoma
子宮内膜症	endometriosis
歯痛	toothache
失語症	aphasia
失神	faint / syncope
湿疹／発疹	rash
しびれ	numbness
自閉症	autism
しもやけ	chilblain
斜視	strabismus
消化不良	indigestion
食中毒	food poisoning
食欲不振	poor appetite
心筋梗塞	myocardial infarction
心身症	psychosomatic disorders
腎臓病	kidney disease
心臓病	heart disease
心臓発作	heart attack
陣痛	labor
心肺停止	cardiac standstill
心不全	heart failure
蕁麻疹	hives
膵臓炎	pancreatitis
睡眠障害	sleep disorder
頭痛	headache
精神異常	insanity
生理痛	period pain

symptoms（病気の症状）

咳	cough	鼻血	bloody nose
摂食障害	eating disorder	鼻づまり	nasal congestion / stuffy nose
全身痙攣	convulsion	鼻水	runny nose
喘息	asthma	腫れ物	swelling
躁病	mania	鼻炎	inflammation of the nose
帯状疱疹	herpes zoster	ヒステリー	hysteria
ダウン症候群	Down's syndrome	肥満	obesity
ただれ	erosion	百日咳	whooping cough
脱水症	dehydration	皮膚炎	dermatitis
窒息	choking	疲労	fatigue
中耳炎	inflammation of the middle ear	貧血	anemia
虫垂炎	appendicitis	風疹	rubella
聴覚障害	deafness	腹痛	stomachache
痛風	gout	腹膜炎	peritonitis
伝染病	epidemic	不妊	sterility
動悸	palpitation	不眠症	insomnia
糖尿病	diabetes mellitus	扁桃炎	tonsillitis
動脈瘤	aneurysm	便秘	constipation
吐血	hematemesis	膀胱炎	cystitis
難聴	hearing-impaired	ポリオ／小児麻痺	polio
にきび	acne	麻痺	paralysis
認知症	dementia	水ぼうそう	chicken pox
熱	fever	水虫	athlete's foot
乳腺炎	inflammation of the mammary	耳鳴り	ringing in the ears
ノイローゼ／神経症	neurosis	耳の痛み	earache
脳卒中	stroke	めまい	dizziness / vertigo
喉の痛み	sore throat	薬疹	drug eruption
吐き気	nausea	腰痛	backache
はしか／麻疹	measles	抑うつ状態	depression
白血病	leukemia	癒着	adhesion

流産	abortion / miscarriage
リュウマチ	rheumatism

Injuries（怪我）

虫刺され	insect bite
むち打ち症	whiplash injury
やけど	burn
裂傷	laceration

Injuries（怪我）

Audio 2-45

あかぎれ	cracks
足首の捻挫	sprained ankle
打ち身	bruise
傷跡	scar
ぎっくり腰	slipped disc
切り傷	cut / wound
筋肉痛	sore muscles
骨折	fracture
こぶ	bump
擦り傷	abrasion
出血	bleeding
脱臼	dislocation
突き指	sprained finger
転倒	falls
床ずれ、褥瘡（じょくそう）	bedsore
内臓破裂	visceral rupture
肉離れ	torn muscle
熱中症	sunstroke
捻挫	sprain
脳震盪	concussion
蜂の刺し傷	beesting
皮下出血	subcutaneous bleeding
日焼け	sunburn
水ぶくれ	blister

I have ～.

Audio 2-46

an ache	痛む
an allergy	アレルギーがある
a bruise	打撲の傷がある
a chill	寒気がする
a cold	風邪をひいている
a cough	咳が出る
a fever	熱がある
the flu	インフルエンザにかかっている
hay fever	花粉症だ
insomnia	不眠症である
a headache	頭痛がする
pneumonia	肺炎に罹っている
a rash	発疹が出ている
a ringing in the ears	耳鳴りがする
a runny nose	鼻水が出る
a sore throat	喉が痛い
a stomachache	お腹が痛い
a stuffy nose	鼻が詰まっている

I feel ～.

Audio 2-47

bad	体の具合が悪い
chilly	寒気がする
cold	寒い
depressed	落ち込んでいる
dizzy	めまいがする
drowsy	うとうとする
embarrassed	恥ずかしい、戸惑う
exhausted	へとへとに疲れている
fatigued	疲弊している
feverish	熱っぽい
good	気分がいい
hungry	お腹がすいている
ill	体調がよくない
irritated	いらいらする
itchy	痒い
lethargic	だるい
nauseous	吐き気がする
numb	しびれている
overwhelmed	圧倒される思いだ
pain	痛む
pleased	うれしい
relieved	ほっとした
sick	気分が悪い
sleepy	眠い
thirsty	のどが渇いた
ticklish	くすぐったい
tired	疲れた
weak	力が入らない
woozy	気分が悪い

不規則動詞の活用表

原形	過去形	過去分詞形	現在分詞形
be [am, is, are]	was, were	been	being
become	became	become	becoming
begin	began	begun	beginning
blow	blew	blown	blowing
break	broke	broken	breaking
bring	brought	brought	bringing
build	built	built	building
burn	burnt, burned	burnt, burned	burning
buy	bought	bought	bought
catch	caught	caught	catching
choose	chose	chosen	choosing
come	came	come	coming
cost	cost	cost	costing
cut	cut	cut	cutting
do [does]	did	done	doing
draw	drew	drawn	drawing
drink	drank	drunk	drinking
drive	drove	driven	driving
eat	ate	eaten	eating
fall	fell	fallen	falling
feed	fed	fed	feeding
feel	felt	felt	feeling
find	found	found	finding
fly	flew	flown	flying
forget	forgot	forgot(ten)	forgetting
freeze	froze	frozen	freezing
get	got	got(ten)	getting
give	gave	given	giving
go	went	gone	going
grow	grew	grown	growing
hang	hung, hanged	hung, hanged	hanging
have [has]	had	had	having
hear	heard	heard	hearing
hide	hid	hid(den)	hiding

原形	過去形	過去分詞形	現在分詞形
hit	hit	hit	hitting
hold	held	held	holding
hurt	hurt	hurt	hurting
keep	kept	kept	keeping
know	knew	known	knowing
lay	laid	laid	laying
lead	led	led	leading
learn	learned, learnt	learned, learnt	learning
leave	left	left	leaving
lend	lent	lent	lending
let	let	let	letting
lie	lay	lain	lying
lose	lost	lost	losing
make	made	made	making
meet	met	met	meeting
pay	paid	paid	paying
put	put	put	putting
read	read	read	reading
ride	rode	ridden	riding
ring	rang	rung	ringing
rise	rose	risen	rising
run	ran	run	running
say	said	said	saying
see	saw	seen	seeing
sell	sold	sold	selling
send	sent	sent	sending
set	set	set	setting
shake	shook	shaken	shaking
show	showed	showed, shown	showing
sing	sang	sung	singing
sit	sat	sat	sitting
sleep	slept	slept	sleeping
smell	smelled, smelt	smelled, smelt	smelling
speak	spoke	spoken	speaking
spend	spent	spent	spending

原形	過去形	過去分詞形	現在分詞形
split	split	split	splitting
spread	spread	spread	spreading
stand	stood	stood	standing
steal	stole	stolen	stealing
sweep	swept	swept	sweeping
swell	swelled	swelled, swollen	swelling
swim	swam	swum	swimming
take	took	taken	taking
teach	taught	taught	teaching
tear	tore	torn	tearing
tell	told	told	telling
think	thought	thought	thinking
throw	threw	thrown	throwing
understand	understood	understood	understanding
wake	woke, waked	woken, waked	waking
wear	wore	worn	wearing
win	won	won	winning
write	wrote	written	writing

代名詞早見表

格 人称・数	主格 (〜は、〜が)	所有格 (〜の)	目的格 (〜を、〜に)	所有代名詞 (〜のもの)	再帰代名詞 (〜自身)
1人称単数	I	my	me	mine	myself
2人称単数	you	your	you	yours	yourself
3人称単数	he	his	him	his	himself
3人称単数	she	her	her	hers	herself
3人称単数	it	its	it	—	itself
1人称複数	we	our	us	ours	ourselves
2人称複数	you	your	you	yours	yourselves
3人称複数	they	their	them	theirs	themselves

JPCA
日本出版著作権協会
http://www.jpca.jp.net/

本書は日本出版著作権協会（JPCA）が委託管理する著作物です。
複写（コピー）・複製、その他著作物の利用については、事前に JPCA（電話 03-3812-9424、e-mail:info@e-jpca.com）の許諾を得て下さい。なお、無断でコピー・スキャン・デジタル化等の複製をすることは著作権法上の例外を除き、著作権法違反となります。

Introduction to Medical English
医療英語入門──医療の現場から日常のシーンまで

2015 年 4 月 5 日　初版　第 1 刷発行
2020 年 4 月10日　第 2 版第 4 刷発行

著　者　稲冨百合子／Dion Clingwall

発行者　森　信久
発行所　株式会社　松 柏 社
〒 102-0072　東京都千代田区飯田橋 1-6-1
TEL　03 (3230) 4813（代表）
FAX　03 (3230) 4857
http://www.shohakusha.com
e-mail: info@shohakusha.com

装　　　幀　小島トシノブ（NONdesign）
本文レイアウト　株式会社クリエーターズ・ユニオン（一柳 茂）
組　　　版　木野内宏行（Alius）
印刷・製本　シナノ書籍印刷株式会社

略号＝ 710
ISBN978-4-88198-710-0
Copyright © 2015 by Yuriko Inadomi & Dion Clingwall

本書を無断で複写・複製することを禁じます。
落丁・乱丁は送料小社負担にてお取り替え致します。